KT-453-425

Conversations:
Christian
and Buddhist

Dom Aelred Graham

Conversations: Christian and Buddhist

Encounters in Japan

Collins
St James's Place   London   1969

First published in the United States of
America 1968 by Harcourt, Brace & World,
Inc., New York

First published in Great Britain 1969 by
William Collins, Sons & Co. Ltd., London

© Aelred Graham, 1968

Printed in Great Britain by
Butler & Tanner Ltd.
Frome and London

Contents

ℵ

"Buddhism in its various forms realizes the radical insufficiency of this changeable world; it teaches a way by which men, in a devout and confident spirit, may be able either to acquire the state of perfect liberation or attain, by their own efforts or through higher help, supreme enlightenment. . . .

"The Church therefore exhorts her sons, that through dialogue and collaboration with the followers of other religions, carried out with prudence and love and in witness to the Christian faith and life, they recognize, preserve and promote the good things, spiritual and moral, as well as the social and cultural values found among these men."

Declaration on the relation of the Church to non-Christian religions,
SECOND VATICAN COUNCIL, 28 *October 1965*

ॷ

Foreword

What follows is in no sense a written work by the author whose
name it bears. It is a piece of reportage owing its existence to a
tape recorder manipulated by a highly competent secretary, who
has used his discretion in abridging and supplying an occasional
indication of the unspoken background to these conversations and
discussions. They are mine only in the sense that I was a leading
participant, having initiated them and to some extent guided their
course. Spontaneity proved to be the rule and scarcely a note was
used by anyone. The interviews took place during a three-month
visit to Japan and are here reproduced in chronological order.

Japan is, I suppose, the most favorable setting in which to observe the living tradition of Mahayana Buddhism. Certainly no
experience could have been more agreeable than the many weeks
spent in the country in which Buddhism is as ancient and deep-
rooted as is the Christianity of the England where I happened to
be born. A kindly providence brought it about that, in my sixtieth
year, having had some lengthy experience of the things of the spirit
in their Catholic expression, I should have the opportunity to meet
and talk with those for whom Sakyamuni the Buddha is no less
significant a figure than is Jesus of Nazareth for the Christian West.

Western missionaries have been in contact with Japan since the sixteenth century, but there are few records of Christians inviting Buddhists to expound their religion in its own terms, or taking Buddhism with the seriousness with which it takes itself. Thus, almost by accident, the ensuing dialogues could have some significance in the history of religion. A book of mine published a few years ago, touching on Zen and its possible application to Catholicism, attracted enough serious, and encouraging, attention to suggest that the matter was worth pursuing further. What I have sought to do is to pass from the area of academic study to that of concrete experience. Here at any rate, it seems to me, is the supremely worthwhile religious encounter: any vital religious discussion in today's world must move, not at the peripheral level of Christian ecclesiology, which still preoccupies so many Catholic theologians, but at the basically existential level of who we are and what human life is all about. Buddhists, like Christians, have their mutual differences and a variety of sects; but if one may risk a generalization, Christians appear to differ fundamentally with regard to superficial matters, whereas Buddhists differ only superficially on that which is fundamental. The drift of my own thought on these topics emerges from the discussions which follow.

It remains only to thank those who made such a rewarding series of dialogues possible. I am most grateful to all those experts in Japan itself—those who live by the message they expounded—who agreed to participate in these conversations. No attempt is made to describe or characterize them, out of deference for the Buddhist ideal that the person who has achieved the great Enlightenment becomes the "true man of no rank." To those who acted as interpreters where the need arose—Professor Masao Abe, Dr. Shojun Bando and, indispensably and in a great variety of contexts, Miss Sumiko Kudo—I wish to express the warmest thanks. Mention should also be made of a number of my fellow Catholic priests. Their words, though not here recorded, fertilized my mind with important elements in the Japanese religious scene: the Jesuit Fathers Heinrich Dumoulin, H. M. Enomiya Lassalle, and Johanne K. Kadowaki, the Carmelite Father I. Okumura, and several Maryknoll Fathers, who were also kind enough to invite me to say Mass at their church during my six weeks' stay in Kyoto. Nor, though in a different category, can I forget my friend Mr. Alan Watts. A "spiritual entertainer," he modestly calls himself; yet I confess myself refreshed by his wit and wisdom, grateful that our paths crossed so congenially while in Japan. A word of gratitude is owing also to the Director and executive staff of the International House of Japan in Tokyo, where my being welcomed as a member made available facilities scarcely otherwise obtainable.

Before leaving Tokyo, on October 10 to be precise, I had the privilege of being invited to lunch at the Okura Hotel by the late Mrs. Ruth Fuller Sasaki, noted Buddhist scholar and the first Westerner admitted to the Rinzai Zen priesthood. She was returning from the United States to her own temple in Kyoto. Though she declined to speak for the record and was clearly in failing health, we conversed freely for nearly four hours. She found time, a few days later, to write a note—one of the last she could have written—from Ryosen-An, Daitoku-ji, to express appreciation of our meeting. It is a touching experience to be able to testify, from another religious tradition, that she bore eloquent and moving witness, so close to the end of her life, to her Zen insight and her unswerving fidelity to the Buddha's message.

Within the United States my sense of indebtedness is widespread. Supporting the venture with their interest and well-wishing were my former associates in the Benedictine Community at Portsmouth Priory in Rhode Island. Their friends proved to be my friends. I think first of Monsignor William J. McCormack of the Archdiocese of New York, who was able and more than willing to volunteer the further support needful on such a "pilgrimage to the East." In the same line of generosity were Mr. and Mrs. Shirley Burden of Beverly Hills, California, Mrs. Francis MacVeagh of St. Helena, California, and Dr. and Mrs. Ciro Scotti of Providence, Rhode Island. The Cambridge (Massachusetts) Buddhist Association, as represented by Miss Misato Toda and Mr. and Mrs. John Mitchell, has played a unique role. Herself a devout Buddhist, Mrs. Mitchell organized the major part of my program in Japan, effecting a number of valuable introductions and assisting the project constructively in innumerable ways, including her help in seeing this book through the press. To these in particular I should like to express a deep sense of gratitude. No one but myself, needless to say, is responsible for passing finally for publication some controversial observations and comments, from various participants, with which others may possibly disagree.

Embarked as I happen to be on observing the practice not only of Mahayana Buddhism, but also of the great non-Christian religions in general, two further names call for grateful acknowledgment. Both were expert advisers on the long term project, with both I had several informative meetings in London before setting out for the Far East. Professor Arnold Toynbee, a friend of thirty years, allowed me to draw freely on his vast stores of knowledge and experience, providing me also with a number of valuable introductions. Likewise Mr. Marco Pallis, the renowned author of *Peaks and Lamas*, deeply committed to a profound religious tradition, has shown a constructive interest in every stage of my journey.

Finally, the warmest appreciation is due to Harold Talbott, who acted as secretary and companion throughout my visit to Japan. He mastered the technique of tape recording and transcribed by hand the material in the pages that follow. The recollection of his past Eastern studies at Harvard, combined with his intense interest in the subjects discussed, has helped to eliminate some of the verbal errors that could easily have crept into the text. Without his persevering industry this book could not have appeared.

AELRED GRAHAM

International House,   *Ampleforth Abbey*
Tokyo, Japan   *York, England*
October 1967   *July 1968*

Conversations: Christian and Buddhist

A Lady First

**Visit of Dom Aelred Graham to Tomiyama Sensei
at her home in Tokyo, August 17, 1967.**

Sumiko Kudo translated.

Tomiyama Sensei, a devout Buddhist, is in charge of Senzan Dormitory, Japan Women's University, where she gives psychological counseling to the students; at the University she lectures on the *Shobo Genzo*. After the exchange of greetings and fond references to Misato Toda, a friend of mine and a student of Tomiyama Sensei, I asked her if it is true that interest in Zen is decreasing in Japan. She replied that since interest in Zen is increasing abroad, young people are beginning to think there may be something in it.

A.G.: Are you a Zen Buddhist?

T.S.: No labels; I am just a Buddhist. In the case of followers of Pure Land, for example, they may prefer to call themselves Pure Land because for them everything is from the other power, that is, from Amida Buddha.

A.G.: Would you say that this distinction between self-power and other power erects a dualism?

T.S.: Yes, but Pure Land aims for humility, which is the final goal of all sects. In the case of Zen, the emphasis is on the true nature or self-nature.

A.G.: How would one recognize a humble person?

T.S.: That is hard to define. It might be possible to point to an example.

A.G.: There is a definition that a humble man is not one who thinks little of self but one who does not think of self at all.

T.S.: Yes. It is not the form, but subjective humbleness which is important.

A.G.: In your experience, would you say that the badly adjusted students are those who have religion or those who do not?

T.S.: Those who do not have any religion have many more problems.

A.G.: And those who get religion wrong have all the more problems.

T.S.: Yes. In that case humility is lost altogether. They have self-assumed images.

A.G.: As with humility, so with truth: the Western mind asks the question "What is truth?"

T.S.: Christianity is very popular among the young intellectuals—they often ask this question. Students without religion also ask.

A.G.: What are they told?

T.S.: They are given abstract explanations at school. When they come to me for counseling, they want to know what the real truth is. "Let's look for it together," I say.

A.G.: Supposing I was looking—what would you say?

T.S.: "Let's look for it together."

A.G.: I am ready to do so!

T.S.: No one can tell whether we will get to the same conclusion or go far apart. But this is the thing we must look for all our life.

A.G.: If Catholicism is properly understood, it has much closer affinities with Buddhism than Protestantism does. For example, Masao Abe goes to Columbia and studies the latest Protestant ideas, but they don't make much sense to him, whereas the great tradition of natural philosophy in Catholicism would have great affinity. Coomaraswamy pointed out that the scholastic philosophers of the Middle Ages were on the same wave length as Hinduism and Buddhism. With the Reformation, Protestant theologians went back to the Hebraic tradition of the Old Testament and there was a break with the tradition of natural philosophy. The Catholic emphasis is that man is a sharer in the Divine Nature, which is close to the Hindu position. Tillich and Suzuki did not see eye to eye because of this very point.

Tomiyama Sensei remarked that she is studying Islam and is going on to study Christianity. She wants to come to the United States in two years, bringing all the questions she has formulated on Christianity. She said that she does not want to study Islam and Christianity from a Buddhist basis, but for what they are in themselves.

A.G.: What are the important questions for me to ask on Buddhism?

T.S.: When I heard from Misato that you were coming to see me, I asked, "For what purpose?" I thought you might like to hear how I lead my everyday life.

A.G.: Yes, but you could not tell in words, could you? I would have to see it minute by minute.

T.S.: I would appreciate it very much.

A.G.: Well, I will ask you a question. What is the meaning of the Zen saying "Emptiness is form and form is emptiness"?

T.S.: When we talk about "emptiness," we refer to reality itself from the viewpoint of its true nature. The fundamental quality is always the same. But we talk about "form" when the true nature of reality exists under varying conditions: phenomenologically speaking, reality is different, and this is what we call "form." As for human beings, the nature of every man is the same as that of every other man, but, according to his surroundings, the appearance of each is different, one from another; when we talk of a particular person, what we see is his outer appearance. The other side of the coin is the fundamental human nature.

A.G.: When we see an individual are we projecting a lot of things which, if we saw through these things, we would find the same emptiness? What does "*Ku*," the emptiness, mean?

T.S.: Psychologically, and this is my personal explanation, one may have the ideal spiritual realm, but in the inner part of his mind he may not really want to be there. But when his possession of the ideal spiritual realm and his desire to be there coincide, then I would call it the state of emptiness. But, on the other hand, if he does not do what he really wants to, this can still be emptiness.

A.G.: Am I right that emptiness is a state of desirelessness? If you desire to be something even very good, it seems to me you are not empty.

T.S.: I told you when these two conditions coincide you are empty: desire does not exist.

A.G.: But couldn't that be bad as well as good? Christianity has too high a view of what should be or what is good, but Zen takes people as they are, good and bad, yang and yin. So wouldn't that just take people as they are?

T.S.: When I try to explain this state of emptiness from the outside, I have to say that such a person who has attained the ideal realm will be just one.

A.G.: The ideal realm will include both good and evil and not be just good?

T.S.: There won't be any struggle; in this person evil can't exist. So there is just one state. Call it good, if you will.

A.G.: According to Catholic philosophy, everything is good: being and good are to some extent coextensive.

T.S.: Yes.

A.G.: There is a Zen saying: "Do not say good, do not say bad."

T.S.: Whoever has attained that level of spirituality will not be emotionally disturbed by evil, even though evil is there.

A.G.: What about "When I first studied Zen, mountains were mountains and waters were waters. While I was studying Zen, mountains were no longer mountains, waters no longer waters. When I had finished studying Zen, mountains were mountains and waters were waters?"

T.S.: First there is just the ordinary statement anyone can make. Then when one views things from the state of emptiness, he expresses the second statement. But then when he comes to know this truth, he does not live in the conceptual knowledge of it but still in the way of everyday life.

I described two fans with these sayings in calligraphy, which Alan Watts had drawn and presented to guests at a dinner. Watts had drawn the circle of emptiness on a fan he presented to me. I referred now to Alan Watts's understanding of the hippies, whom he considers a kind of parallel to the early Christians.

A.G.: The American society has betrayed them; they have nothing to look forward to, because they are not interested in the rewards of industrial society—they are horrified by the Vietnam war—and so they get out of the society and live for the moment, without working and without money and without thought for the morrow. This is pretty closely linked with drugs—LSD—since they find so little to interest them in the society that they take an inward trip.

S.K.: There is a confusion between Zen and drugs in some minds here and in the United States. Dr. Suzuki suggested I take LSD and tell him about it.

A.G.: I'm getting tired myself with all this cerebration. It has been a great pleasure being here.

T.S.: Thank you. You mentioned in your letter you were interested in seeing Misato's teacher. Whatever good points she has are her own, and I didn't necessarily have anything to do with it!

Conversation between Professor Masao Abe
and Dom Aelred Graham in Kyoto, August 26, 1967.

I showed Professor Abe the two fans on which Alan Watts had drawn designs: on one the characters for "Form is emptiness" and on the other the circle representing Sunyata, or "*Ku*." Of the latter Abe asked, "What is this?" "Emptiness" was my reply.

M.A.: "Emptiness" is not emptiness itself.
A.G.: No.
M.A.: So, what is emptiness itself? Not in words.
A.G.: It is only to be experienced—it cannot be described.
M.A.: But you describe it in the term of "indescribability."
A.G.: Ineffability. Yes. It cannot be spoken.
M.A.: But . . . you are still speaking.
A.G.: Therefore . . . silence.
M.A.: You said, "Silence." That's not silence; it's not actual silence. . . . What is the true silence, or true emptiness?

There was a long pause.

M.A.: Thank you very much.
A.G.: Thank *you*.

The conversation then turned to the subject of Alan Watts.

A.G.: Have you ever met him?

M.A.: Yes, I've met him a few times.

A.G.: What do you think of his understanding of Zen?

M.A.: It's a very difficult question to answer.

A.G.: Perhaps it's a question of his having an insight of his own, rather than the orthodox Zen insight. Do you think that could be true?

M.A.: I think he's a very clever man, clever interpreter of Zen, but I don't know how much he has practiced Zen meditation.

A.G.: Not much, I don't think; but one can't be sure.

M.A.: Maybe not.

A.G.: I think he doesn't believe very much in Zazen, though he has profound insight, brilliantly expressed. What would be your feeling about a person who didn't believe very much in Zazen? Aren't there some Buddhists who don't believe in Zazen—is that right, could that be?

M.A.: Zazen in a sense is not absolutely necessary. What is important is Enlightenment, not Zazen. However, generally speaking, Zazen is a very necessary and important practice of Zen realization.

A.G.: We do a little Zazen here each day, sometimes twice a day. Harold was asking me what benefit comes from doing Zazan half an hour, say, each day. What would you say to that?

M.A.: By the practice of Zazen we concentrate ourselves so that we can come to mental concentration even when we're doing something else—reading a book, walking down a street, or doing business and so forth. We can concentrate ourselves through daily practice of Zazen. This may be one of the practical benefits.

A.G.: Do you think it has the effect of calming the spirit?

M.A.: Yes. I think concentration of mind is useful in doing anything. When we read a book, if we can really concentrate ourselves on doing so, we can understand much better. Concentration of mind will be easily achieved through Zazen practice.

A.G.: To come to your own studies of Christianity: you have spent a good deal of time at Columbia and elsewhere. Would you say that there are any links between Christianity and Zen? We had somebody telling us the other day in Tokyo that a famous lady in these parts, Ruth Fuller Sasaki, takes the view, or has expressed the view, that there is no possibility of a fusion, no real link between Christianity and Zen Buddhism. What would be your comment on that?

M.A.: I think there is something that is common, that may be a bridge between them, particularly in practice. Last April I participated in a colloquium on Christianity and Zen Buddhism held by a Quaker, Dr. Steer, near Tokyo, at Oiso Academy House. Fathers Dumoulin and Lassalle attended. You should meet Lassalle—he is living in Hiroshima. I was very interested in knowing him. He is, of course, a very pious Christian father, and he has practiced Zazen. The Soto Zen Master Harada Sogaku has been his teacher for the last ten years or so. Every winter he went to Harada Sogaku's temple to participate in Sesshin, intensive meditation week. And he said that he was qualified by the Zen Master, that he got Enlightenment.

A.G.: The master said that he achieved Kensho, or Satori?

M.A.: Yes. And Father Lassalle told me that he could reach a much deeper dimension of the mind through Zazen practice than by Catholic prayer. He said that before Zazen practice he could come to a certain depth of mind through Catholic meditation, but to him there was some hindrance he could not break through; but when he practiced Zazen he could break through or go beyond that hindrance or wall. So for him Zazen meditation is very helpful for his Catholic way of meditation. Of course he will never give up the Catholic way; rather, he takes Zen meditation into his spiritual life. Recently he is guiding his student followers, who are of course Catholic believers, by encouraging them to do Zazen and Dokusan. You know Dokusan, don't you?

A.G.: That is going to the Zen Master with a koan.

M.A.: Yes, a personal interview with the Zen Master.

A.G.: And is he the, kind of, Catholic Zen Master?

M.A.: He is a Catholic Father in Zen style.

H.T.: Does he hold the Dokusan himself?

M.A.: Yes. He uses the method of Dokusan in his teaching, guiding his students to come to the Catholic faith.

A.G.:   And what do you think about it?

M.A.:   I think, at least for him—according to my impression—it is
a very successful way. And I understand that he does not give up
the Catholic way, but, rather, deepens his way by Zen meditation. And he said that there is no contradiction in that way at all.
I would recommend that you talk with him about this, so you
may have direct information.

A.G.:   Yes, I would like very much to, because I see certain difficulties arising from what exactly is the content of his Enlightenment experience and to what extent he is tied to a form of meditation devised by the founder of the Jesuit order, Saint Ignatius
Loyola. I would question a bit. I would like to ask to see him and
ask him questions. Harold read the book rather carefully—would
you care to say something about it?

H.T.:   I think it's a clear and mostly experiential account of what
Zen is, mostly through Father Lassalle's own experiences in Sesshin and observations of the Zen monasteries. He describes meditation and what Zen is as far as it can be expressed verbally. My
impression is that he then almost states the Catholic, particularly
the Jesuit, point of view, that there is a distinction between religions that have an understanding of natural philosophy. But that
Zen does not possess the Catholic understanding of the supernatural order, which comes through Revelation, and that it is
not available to them. So, after giving what appears to be an
accurate introductory account of Zen, he goes on to say that it is
merely a natural philosophy, without the Enlightenment of the
supernatural order. Dom Aelred speculates that this is a way of
writing books to get by the censor in heavily disciplined orders
like the Jesuit. It would be interesting to know when Father
Lassalle wrote the book, in relation to when the Zen Master Harada said that he achieved this deep understanding of Zen—because he may not hold those views any longer. Interestingly
enough, Father Dumoulin said that all the Zen Masters he had
spoken to deny that Father Lassalle had achieved any sort of
Kensho. They admire him as a good Catholic priest. Father
Dumoulin expected that some time the Zen Masters would

affirm that Father Lassalle had achieved Kensho, but then when he spoke to them, he decided that they would never accept Father Lassalle's Enlightenment. An interesting contradiction. Father Dumoulin denied that the distinction between the natural and the supernatural order existed in the book, and he suggested that perhaps I had misread it.

A.G.: During several of our discussions with other people on Zen, the technical term "Inka" has come up. Can you tell us anything about what that means?

M.A.: "Inka" means official certification given by a master to a disciple who is considered by the master to have achieved Enlightenment.

A.G.: It doesn't give the disciple a right to teach? It doesn't constitute him a Roshi?

M.A.: Not necessarily.

A.G.: Is it an official, external document, or is it a private thing?

M.A.: It's a private thing. So the master never announces publicly whether he gives Inka to one or another, because such a certification has been done rather secretly between the master and the disciple. So no one knows. . . .

A.G.: Whether somebody has Inka or not?

M.A.: Yes. It should not be talked about easily or in an open way. There is a case in which a master left in his will after his death the designation of whom he gave Inka to.

A.G.: By what standards does a Zen Master decide whether somebody has received Enlightenment or not?

M.A.: It is clear and definite. As you know, in the monastery, besides sitting in meditation, Dokusan is a very important practice —that is, the way of giving koans to disciples. The disciple presents to the master the view on a koan that he has reached through his meditation and his laboring on the question. This koan practice continues for many years. They have a personal interview almost every day in their monastic life. Sometimes they have a personal interview four or five times a day during Sesshin, intensive meditation week. And by examining the view presented by the disciple, the master can judge how deeply he understands or experiences Zen. So the master always has a very close observation of the disciple's practice and experience. After several years' practice, if someone comes to the final understanding point of his experience and presents it to the master in the proper way, then the master can see it. He can judge whether this man has attained . . .

A.G.: But what is the master looking for in the disciple? He must have some preconceived notion of what he's looking for in any particular disciple.

M.A.: He gives various koans to confirm his disciple's experience. There are also many variations of one koan. For instance, one of the most famous koans is Mu. So the master first gives the koan What is Mu? After some period of laboring on this koan Mu, the disciple may come to the point where he can present the proper view of this koan, and the Master agrees to his view. Even then the Master usually gives him variations of the koan Mu. For instance, "Stand Mu up!" or "What is the back side of Mu?" or "Let Mu walk!" and so forth. There are many variant forms of one important koan. So even when a disciple passes one particular koan successfully, the master gives a variation of that and tries to check whether the disciple's experience is genuine or not by observing him from various angles. If the disciple does not understand that koan profoundly enough, he may not show the proper view on the variation.

A.G.: I think I get something of the picture. It depends a great deal on the experience and skill of the Roshi, I would think, doesn't it—to be able to make those judgments?

M.A.: The Roshi has genuine experience of Enlightenment, and he will know the function of that realization, so he can judge by observing the disciple's view whether he has the same experience.

A.G.: To change the topic for the moment, would you say yes or no, or what sort of answer would you give, to the question "Is Zen a religion?" Is that a koan?

M.A.: May I ask you, what do you mean by "religion"?

A.G.: By "religion" I mean some process whereby man relates himself to a Reality that he regards as greater and more significant than himself.

M.A.: Reality . . .

A.G.: Reality, yes—with a capital R.

M.A.: I would say that Zen is a religion in your sense.

A.G.: Would you say that it's a religion in the sense that Christianity is a religion?

M.A.: What do you have in your mind when you say "Christianity"?

A.G.: I was trying to draw you out on your observations and studies of Christianity—the form of Christianity that must have been presented to you in your studies in the West. My understanding was that those studies were rather in terms of modern Protestant theologians like Karl Barth, perhaps, and Tillich and Bultmann, and people like that, and I wondered what links or what similarities or dissimilarities you found—you have written something on those themes—between their presentations and your own understanding of the Buddhist tradition. Perhaps that's too big a question.

M.A.: Yes, it's a really big question. I said that Zen is a religion because you said that religion is a realization of Reality. . . .

A.G.: Relating oneself, I think I used—feeling a sense of relation to some ultimate Reality greater than oneself—God, it's called by the Christians.

M.A.: As you know, Nietzsche negated Christianity, but he negated the so-called "Christendom," not necessarily Jesus himself. He negated, if I'm not wrong, the established form of Christianity, but not Jesus himself. So if you mean the "Christendom" or established Christianity by the term "Christianity" . . .

Professor Abe's line of argument was interrupted by dinner.

A.G.: Do you know a Miss Carmen Blacker?

M.A.: I met her only a few times—so we are not so intimate.

A.G.: She teaches Japanese, I think, at Cambridge University.

M.A.: Yes. She published a book on Fukuzawa Yukichi, one of the outstanding pioneer thinkers of the Meiji reform.

A.G.: So she is a learned lady.

M.A.: She is interested in Japanese folk religion as well as Zen.

A.G.: It is said she has walked on fire and not come to any harm. . . . What are the important things to be seen in Kyoto?

M.A.: First of all, you should see Dr. Hisamatsu, my teacher. He is a genuine Zen man. He is not a priest, but a layman. But in my view he is a much more profound and genuine Zen man than any master, and he has a very deep Zen realization, as well as a philosophical mind. His teacher was the late Kitaro Nishida, who is the most outstanding Japanese philosopher after the Meiji restoration. Hisamatsu studied philosophy with him and practiced Zazen seriously in the monastery of Myoshin-ji Temple. He is really a great man, with a profound realization of Zen, and an excellent talent for calligraphy, the tea ceremony, and so forth. However, he is now not well; he is weak. He is now seventy-eight years old. So I will make an appointment for you to see him a little before you leave Kyoto.

H.T.: Dr. Hisamatsu is the founder of the Cambridge Buddhist Association, in Massachusetts.

M.A.: Yes, he is. He was a visiting professor at the Harvard Divinity School.

A.G.: And he knows Mrs. Mitchell.

M.A.: Yes. He often attended the meditation meeting at the Mitchells' house. And I would recommend that you meet Professor Keiji Nishitani. He is also one of my old teachers. He is a professor of religious philosophy and a member of the Japanese Academy. He has a good understanding of Western philosophy, particularly Western mysticism—Plotinus, Meister Eckhart, Jacob Boehme and others.

A.G.: Does he know English?

M.A.: Yes, he knows English, German, French, Latin, and others.

A.G.: And he teaches in Kyoto, does he?

M.A.: Yes, he does. He retired from Kyoto University and is now teaching at Otani University. He is one of the most eminent philosophers of Japan today. His basic standpoint is Buddhism, in particular Zen, while he has a wide and good understanding of Western traditions. So I think it would be interesting for you to meet him.

A.G.: What are the active Zen Buddhist monasteries nearby?

M.A.: Did Miss Kudo arrange for you to meet Shibayama Roshi? [He is the Abbot of Nanzen-ji. Masao Abe and Sumiko Kudo agree that Shibayama Roshi and Morimoto Roshi are the two most celebrated Zen Masters of Japan today.]

A.G.: Yes. She is taking us to see him.

M.A.: He is a Zen Master whom you shouldn't miss. And another Zen Master is Shonen Morimoto. He was originally a layman. He is interested in Pure Land Buddhism as well as Zen, so his position is unique among Zen Masters.

A.G.: Isn't it true to say that Mrs. Mitchell is interested in Zen but also in the cultus of Amida—isn't that the Pure Land?

M.A.: Mrs. Mitchell is interested in that, too?

A.G.: It seems so to me. She is not just content to sit in Zazen. She has the need for a quite active life, of the cultic bhakti side.

M.A.: Whom are you planning to see besides Shibayama?

A.G.: We're going to the Reverend Tetsuya Inoue at Eiten-ji.

M.A.: I think that temple is located behind the mountain near Kobe. Is that a temple Mrs. Mitchell recommended that you visit?

A.G.: Yes. The one she spent a lot of time at was Eihei-ji. That's a long way away, isn't it?

M.A.: Yes. It's located deep in the mountains a little way from Fukui. Eihei-ji is another place you should not miss.

A.G.: That was Dogen's temple.

M.A.: Dogen's temple, yes.

A.G.: Were these temples and monasteries interfered with during the war or the occupation by American troops? Was the life interrupted? Were the monks disturbed?

M.A.: Not disturbed in an official way by the army. But the Shinto shrines were interrupted in their religious activities by the occupation army, because Shinto was regarded as something political and militaristic.

A.G.:   Are there Buddhist convents of nuns?

M.A.:   Yes. There is a school for nuns in Kyoto established by one of the Pure Land sects. I have a close friend of that sect, and I'll be pleased to introduce you to him if you want to see the nunnery.

A.G.:   Are there many sisters there?

M.A.:   Not so many. Recently the number has diminished. There is also a Zen monastery for nuns in Kyoto.

A.G.:   And are there female Roshis?

M.A.:   Yes, female Roshis, perhaps. It's not important to become a Roshi, but to become enlightened.

A.G.:   It's the same with Christianity: it's not important to be a priest or a monk, but it's important to be a good Christian.

M.A.:   Yes, surely. I may be wrong. But anyhow, there is a female temple master.

A.G.:   Temple mistress.

M.A.:   Do you have a female prior?

A.G.:   Prioresses. Oh, yes. Very many.

H.T.:   The Prioress—a famous character in the *Canterbury Tales* of Chaucer.

M.A.:   And Saint Teresa, no? There are many woman mystics— *Frauen mystiker* in the West.

A.G.:   Oh yes. "The devout feminine sex," it says in the Catholic liturgy.

M.A.:   Could you tell me something about hippies?

A.G.:   Harold can tell you about the hippies?

H.T.:   Well, back to Alan Watts. We ran into him in San Francisco; he is authoritative on the hippies. He knows many and has a lot of sympathy for them. He has formulated a systematic definition of what the hippies are. Then he said we must look up the Japanese version of hippies. We asked a friend here if there were any Japanese hippies, and she said no. Others have said there are. Dom Aelred has had experience with hippies. He knows a few, and he got on very well with them. Recently a Japanese newspaper reported on them. Something like American hippies appeared in Tokyo, near Shinjuku. They are indifferent to social problems, and they wear very sloppy clothes; they look

c

very idle. And the newspaper says that these young boys and girls may be influenced by American hippies, though American hippies emphasize not fighting but love.

A.G.: "Make love, not war."

H.T.: They have large gatherings in parks, called "love-ins," and they recite the *Hannya-shin-gyo*.

M.A.: Are they somewhat religious?

H.T.: They have a sense.

A.G.: They get up and go and sit in Zazen at four-thirty in the morning at the Zendo, on Bush Street in San Francisco, under the Reverend Suzuki.

M.A.: I visited that Zen center. Do hippies attend the Zazen meetings?

A.G.: Yes, they go there!

H.T.: Robert Aitken, in Hawaii—he has a Zendo, and a lot of hippies come to him. He says that often when hippies begin to sit in Zazen, they stop taking LSD, because they feel they get what they need from Zazen and they don't have to take any more LSD. It's not an escape, but a vision, that they think the drug gives them, so they stop that and sit in Zazen.

M.A.: So they're serious in that sense, are they?

H.T.: They have a philosophical basis for their way of life. And, Dom Aelred—I think you feel they're not insincere?

A.G.: No. I think they're witnessing to something—particularly in America, where there's really not much sense of tradition, the way there is in this country. The American way of life is to look to the future, not to the past. But these hippies—they're very disillusioned with the way things have gone in America, particularly with regard to civil rights, that nothing really effective is being done about the Negroes, that nothing is being done to make life more tolerable in the cities for poor people, and that we've involved ourselves in an impossible situation in Vietnam. . . .

Harold is interested, as everybody is, in the breakthrough from conceptual thinking and verbal expression to something beyond that. Could you say something about that? Although you can't say what is the meaning of Mu or nothingness. It's just a question—isn't it—of experience, and those who know don't say and those who say don't know—isn't that it?

M.A.: I'm sorry, I don't follow you quite.

A.G.: Well—if Harold can put his difficulty again.

H.T.: We should tell Professor Abe what we were talking about today—the principle that Thomas Aquinas worked out about relationship. I've been reading Conze recently, and he uses the term "the absolute" in that book: he is trying to give some impression in conceptual terms of what Buddhism is concerned with. Dom Aelred suggests that "the absolute" is a Western term that doesn't have very much correspondence to Buddhism. Conze remarks that nirvana has no relation to contingent reality; therefore you cannot do anything to attain nirvana and you cannot say anything about nirvana. But at a certain level you have to adopt particular references to nirvana that are ultimately false, but that get you somewhere at a certain stage. Dom Aelred thought this was too simple a way of talking in a paragraph of something of great importance. Then he talked about Thomas Aquinas on ultimate reality.

A.G.: He takes the view about the ultimate reality, which we call God, that it is more profitable to talk in negative terms than in positive terms. We know more about what God is not than about what he is. Thomas derived a good deal of that doctrine from a Western theologian-philosopher, Dionysius the Areopagite. And Conze suggests that the doctrine goes back to the Upanishads, sixth century B.C. I was very interested to see that, because it's a link between Eastern and Western thought that must have struck a lot of people as possible, but Conze seems to be much more emphatic and suggests that there's actual evidence. Thomas maintains that you cannot say that God is related, that there's any real relation in God, to human beings, although in view of the doctrine of creation, you can say that there's a real relation of creatures to God. Much as you can say that when sunlight falls on a certain patch of ground, nothing happens to the sun—there's no modification of the sun—so that the sun is not related to that piece of ground, although there's a modification in the piece of ground; it is related to the sun— something in those terms. It's a metaphysical and abstract line of thought, if you like, but it seems to me to be nearer to Hindu and Buddhist insight than a good deal of this modern Christian theology, which goes back to the Bible, a very anthropomorphic document, thinking of God in man-made terms. And that is why I've often suggested—I think I suggested it in some comments on an essay of yours—that there's a much closer link between the underlying philosophy of Catholicism and Hinduism, Buddhism, and Zen than there is between modern Protestant theology and those Eastern traditions. But the actual thing you're hankering after, Harold, is a question of experience, rather than study, and the "emptiness"—we just flickered on it at the beginning with Professor Abe—is lost as soon as you start to talk about it. In experiential terms I take it to mean the non-attachment that makes you transparent, as it were, to every experience, to all reality, so that there are no blocks and there is no substance put in the way. You're just empty. It's the same as a certain fullness, too.

M.A.: Negative theology, the Via Negativa, has some similarity to the Buddhist position. As you said, the ultimate reality cannot be described in positive terms. We can indicate it only by saying it is *not* so and so. This does not mean that the absolute, or ultimate reality, has no relationship to relative reality. At least in Buddhism, if the absolute is not related to the relative, it is not the true absolute.

A.G.: Well, my query would be: Does Buddhism really admit the absolute? Isn't that a Western term? Is there anything in Buddhist terminology that corresponds to "the absolute"? The Buddhist canonical scriptures speak of the unborn and unseen, and if it were not for that unborn and unseen, there would be no way to escape from the born and the seen, and so on. But that seems to me a much subtler way of expressing the doctrine than in terms of the absolute and the relative. As I understand it, the Buddhist

way of thinking is very much in terms of interrelation of everything with everything else, and that nirvana is not an attaining
of the absolute, but an attaining of a certain emptiness, so that
one realizes this interrelationship of everything with everything
else. By "realize" I mean that you become it—*Tat tvam asi*. Am
I talking correctly?

M.A.: Yes. One of the basic principles of Buddhism is pratitya
samutpada, which is Sanskrit, and may be translated as "dependent co-ordination" or "dependent . . ."

A.G.: "Co-inherence"?

M.A.: "Well, dependently co-ordinated origination": everything
is interdependently related in its origination. So there is no
independent thing that has nothing to do with others. There is
not in Buddhism the only one, substantial ultimate principle,
the absolute, even in terms of God, or creator, or so forth. So
if there is the one God from which everything comes out and
to which everything returns, Buddhism should ask: Is that only
God *really* absolute? Because there's some relative relationship
between God as creator and men as creation. Dr. Suzuki once
raised a very interesting question to a Christian guest: "In Genesis in the Old Testament it is written, 'And God said let there
be light: and there was light.' Who heard and recorded this
word of God when he said this? Unless there was someone who
listened and witnessed God saying let there be light, these words
would not have been recorded in Genesis. Who is the witness?"
Could you answer this question?

A.G.: I could say what is usually said about it these days: that the
story is poetic, mythological, and that the writer of it, or the
source from which it came, was concerned with giving an account
of how the world came to be. So, by an act of the imagination, he
produced this poetry. Just as the myth of the origin of Japan is
that a god and goddess got together and produced the beautiful
island of Japan, and then as a kind of afterthought gave birth to
the sun, so that the sun came into being just to light up Japan.
That's very nice poetry. Genesis is much the same, don't you
think?

M.A.: Of course the Genesis story is mythological. However, it is something more than mythology, I think. It implies religious faith in God as creator. That is essential to Christianity.

A.G.: Well, the mature Christian might ask: "What do you mean by faith and what do you mean by creation?" But it's the truth that for the average workaday Christian your statement is correct.

M.A.: So we need not take this mythological story in its literal sense?

A.G.: I don't think so.

M.A.: But the religious reality implied in it should not be overlooked. And in my understanding, Dr. Suzuki's question is directed to a concealed witness to the relationship between God as creator and the world as creation. The divine-human relationship in creation is fundamental in Christianity, and Suzuki's question is concerned with what is the basis of this particular relationship as such. So far as there is a divine-human relationship there must be a basis for the relationship; in other words, there must be something deeper than the divine-human relationship as such. On what basis can this divine-human relationship take place? This is a question with which Zen is seriously concerned. For example, the Zen Master Joshu was once asked by his disciple, "When everything is reduced to one, what is that oneness reduced to?" If the final understanding is that everything is reduced to one, there is still a relativity or a relationship between one and many.

A.G.: I think many Western logicians and thinkers would say there is an ultimate basis or premise beyond which you cannot go. That is the starting point. It is self-evident, a postulate of human thinking, they would say. Therefore, you can't go beyond that; it just is. Isn't there a parallel to that in Buddhism? For instance, if you say, as I believe Buddhists do, that the Buddha nature is in everyone, what do you reply if I ask, "What is the basis for that statement?" Isn't that an ultimate statement? You can only know that by experience, can't you? No amount of logic could persuade anyone of it. Isn't that so?

M.A.: About the Christian statement "God is the only creator" and the Buddhist statement "Everyone has a Buddha nature"— both statements can be really understood only through experience. It's clear. However, what understanding of the truth is implied in these statements beyond experience is another question.

A.G.: I think it important to have these experiences and to recognize that only through experience are these basic things going to be realized. At the same time, it is part of the civilized process, and very important for doctrinal teaching purposes, to try to explain such matters in conceptual and verbal terms. I think that that is what religious teachers and philosophers in the past have done in the Hindu, Buddhist, and Christian traditions.

M.A.: Yes. So the religious truth that is beyond conceptual understanding must be deep enough not to be destroyed by any intellectual analysis.

A.G.: That's right.

M.A.: In that sense, although you say it is a premise for a Westerner that God is the only creator, this should be argued and stood up to critical examination.

A.G.: I agree. For instance, Thomas Aquinas would say, or, rather, offer argumentation for the fact, that the world is dependent on something other than itself, that it doesn't account for its own existence. He argues for that at length; but those arguments are not convincing to everybody nowadays. Within the framework of that kind of thinking, the arguments were quite consistent and well formulated. Metaphysics, however, has been described as the finding of good arguments for what you believe on instinct.

M.A.: On the meaning of the phrase "ultimate truth," the question is: What is the ground for speaking of ultimate truth? If there is no basis for ultimate truth, then it appears to be a concept based on our uncritical assumption. So it cannot be said to be ultimate truth or ultimate reality, for we must try to go behind any kind of assumption before we can reach ultimate reality. That is the reason why Buddhism does not admit the one God as creator.

A.G.:   That is very impressive and hard to refute. The theologians
say that there are certain things *per se nota*, self-evident; they
maintain, many of them, that all gain knowledge through the
senses, that all our ideas come through the senses. They would
say that that is a fact of experience; it is not an assumption, they
would say. This is self-evident. Those who deny it cannot maintain their denial without implicitly acknowledging what they
profess to deny. You would probably challenge that. It is a position that takes a view of human knowledge different from that
which began with Descartes. Modern philosophers take the view
that thought comes first, and being, reality, comes afterward;
whereas a different school takes the view that being, reality,
comes first and thought afterward. Thus, according to this latter
view, thought conforms to being, not vice versa; whereas modern
philosophers and those Christian theologians you have been
largely influenced by regard thought as a sort of creative process
—that to some extent you create your own reality. Here, I believe, there is no bridging of the gap between thought and reality. Thus these thinkers are free to challenge every proposition
and to say that every statement you make is an assumption. On
the basis of their own philosophy it would be hard to refute
them. The question resolves itself, it seems to me, into: What is
the origin of our ideas and what is the nature of knowledge? My
feeling is that the Buddhist epistemology is much nearer to that
of Plato, Aristotle, and Thomas than it is to Descartes, Kant,
and Hegel.

M.A.:   Yes. The question is: *Who* takes it as self-evident when you
say that some final statement is self-evident?

A.G.:   Not the *final* statement, but the *initial* statement. Thomas
would say that *there is movement*. That is self-evident. If people
deny that, well, you can't get any further.

M.A.:   But who does recognize that everything is moving?

H.T.:   Modern philosophers would say that that is an assumption
that cannot be proved; it cannot be stated with any meaning.
Any logical positivist would say that the statement "There is
movement" does not have logical content; it has no descriptive
bearing on reality.

M.A.: Whether you may deny or affirm that everything is moving —*who* does so affirm or so negate that everything is moving?

A.G.: I don't think our statement takes the form that "everything is moving." That could not be established without a cosmic knowledge of particulars. The statement is: "Things move," "anything moves," "one thing moves." Harold's point is a good one about the logical positivists and linguistic analysts—their insistence on non-meaningfulness. But their position amounts to a sort of dogmatic skepticism, which you can't do much about. So when you're debating matters in that climate of opinion, it seems to me that you have to say, not "What does that mean?" or, "What content do you attach to that?" but "Why do you say that? What leads you to say that?" Meaning is a question of semantics, but the question "Why?" brings you, or links you, to the existential world.

H.T.: Professor Abe, when you asked "What leads you to deny or affirm anything?" were you asking about some particular thinkers?

M.A.: No. I'm asking: When you say there is movement, or everything is the creation of God, what is the relation between the speaker and that very statement? Where do you find yourself in such a statement? Do you find yourself in every created thing? Or in God as creator? Or somewhere else? That is the point of Suzuki's question to his guest about Genesis. Who was the witness when God said "Let there be light," and there was light?

A.G.: I think that when one is pressed—and it is a very important question—one is obliged to say: It seems to me, or it seems, that there is a creator God. And if that were further analyzed: Such consciousness as I may be said to have testifies to certain phenomena from which by a process of inference I feel justified in positing the existence of an ultimate reality that we call God.

M.A.: What are you talking about when you say "God"?

A.G.: We are using the word "God" because it seems to the observer to apply to a reality more fundamental than any other object of experience. I think one would say that you do not find yourself in that statement at all—except indirectly.

M.A.: You do not find yourself in that statement?

A.G.:   No.

M.A.:   But, who is saying "You do not find yourself in the statement?" What of you says so when you say so?

A.G.:   What of you? That question could be asked of any statement, it seems to me.

M.A.:   Surely.

A.G.:   If you say, "Form is emptiness, emptiness is form," you could ask the same question about anybody who says that, couldn't you? Why do you? What leads any individual to make that statement? You challenge me to say what of you there is in the statement "There is a creator God." Cannot I say, "What of you is in the statement that form is precisely emptiness, emptiness is form"? If you agree to that statement.

M.A.:   It's Emptiness. It's Nothing, and neither God nor everything, but Nothing.

H.T.:   And that's the answer to "What of you is in that statement?"

M.A.:   Yes.

A.G.:   Very thought-provoking.

H.T.:   What did Suzuki's Christian visitor say?

M.A.:   Oh, he didn't mention what the visitor said, and I do not know Suzuki's final statement in this connection. But I would say to his question—"Who listened to and recorded God's voice?"—there is Nothing. But this Nothing or void or Sunyata is the basis for both God and his creation. So this Nothingness is not mere void or Nothing, but most fundamental Nothingness or creative void, from which even God and his creation springs.

H.T.:   How about the origin of the universe in the Hindu myth of the dance of Shiva?

M.A.:   As you know, in Hinduism Atman and Brahman are one. But Sakyamuni raised the question "What does oneness really mean? On what basis can we talk about the oneness of Atman and Brahman?" So Sakyamuni came to the point of Anatman, or non-self—no ego. It's the negation of Atman, which is one with Brahman. And to the Zen question "When everything is reduced to one, what is that one reduced to?" the answer may be "nothing" or may be "everything" *at the same time*. So, in other words, it is *both* nothing and everything.

A.G.: What is? What is the "it" that is both nothing and everything?

M.A.: It is that to which, ultimately, "one" may be reduced. Both nothing and everything and *at the same time* neither nothing nor everything. That is the void in the Buddhist sense—as Alan Watts put on your fan: Form as it is is void; void as it is is form. This is just another expression of the same thing I said right now about that to which the ultimate one is reduced. This is my rather logical explanation.

A.G.: Yes. I think I'll have to go through several Sesshins before I can rise to that.

M.A.: There is a story of ancient India. Once there was a young fellow named Yajnadatta. He was a very handsome youth, so he would look in a mirror every morning to see his image reflected, and he would smile at his own image. One morning his face was not reflected in the mirror. He was really surprised and upset, and he thought that his head was lost. He looked for his head. "Where is my head? Where is my head?" And he searched for his head everywhere, but he couldn't find it anywhere. Finally he came to realize that the head for which he was searching was nothing but the head doing the searching. The careless fellow had looked at the rear of the mirror, and naturally his head was not reflected. His head was not lost, but since he looked at the back of the mirror he thought it was lost. And he looked for his head with his head. So the more he looked for his head externally, the more he went contrariwise. His head was not something that could be found in front of him, but it was here! It is always here, verily on his side. But he looked for his head externally with his head, and the more he did so, the more he went astray. My living head can never be seen by myself. It can never be objectified by myself. My head may have form from your viewpoint, but no form from mine. In other words, my head is nothing for me, because it never can be objectified, can never be an object for me. In that sense it is not something, but nothing. However, it is nothing not because there is no head for me, but the contrary, because it is *my own living head*. It is not an object of my objectification, but the ground of my objectification. So it is true for you: Do you see your own head?

A.G.:   I see what you're saying. I follow—at least I think I follow what you're saying.

≥ *The Fountainhead*

Visit of Dom Aelred Graham
to the Reverend Kobori Sohaku at his sub-temple
at Daitoku-ji Monastery, Kyoto, September 2, 1967.

Sumiko Kudo was also present.

A.G.: We were given some fans when we were in San Francisco.
K.S.: Take off your coats perhaps.
S.K.: Yes, you will be more comfortable that way.
A.G.: Oh, that would be nice. (I handed my fan to Kobori San.)
Perhaps you can explain what that means. (On the fan is drawn
the circle of Sunyata.)
S.K.: Mr. Alan Watts.
K.S.: Oh . . . oh. Zen Master. Watts has visited here several
times.
A.G.: And this is Harold's. (On it are written the characters for
"Form is emptiness.")
S.K.: Also written by Mr. Watts.
K.S.: I hope you will explain the meaning. I don't know!
A.G.: I have come all the way to Japan to find out.
K.S.: I don't know the meaning. It is taken from scripture, a very
famous saying. He is quite good at calligraphy, Mr. Watts. The
fan is too little for you—you need a much bigger one.
A.G.: I have come to Japan, though not to get involved in the
Catholic missionary side of things. When I was in the West, in
America, I tried to write something to illuminate Christianity,

Catholicism, from the Buddhist point of view as I understood it
—and I am just beginning to understand it perhaps a little—because it seems to me that Western Christianity is very much in
need of that kind of insight. From what I learn of history, the
contacts of Christian, Catholic, missionaries with Hinduism and
Buddhism have not been a very happy thing, because the missionaries felt they had come to these very old, civilized religions
with a message to deliver and very little to learn. That seems to
me a great pity, and is working out now, I think, in the fact that
the Christian message, even for the West, doesn't have all the
answers, doesn't have the solution to a good many problems. To
my understanding, a good deal of light could be thrown onto the
Christian, particularly the Catholic, standpoint from the Zen insight. It's that that I have come to learn about. So that it's literally true when I say it's *that* [the statement "Form is emptiness"] I have come to learn about. I'm not particularly interested in dialogue—the exchange of ideas for their own sake—
that can go on indefinitely, and neither side is convinced or persuaded. That's just an exchange of a lot of concepts, words. I
come in the office of someone anxious to learn, to have Buddhism expounded from its authentic source. I have no inclina-
tion at present, and I don't expect ever to have one, to change
allegiances; but I think, and have felt for nearly forty years,
that so far as I have touched on these things, the quieter, more
profound insight of Buddhism is more illuminating in many
ways than the involved historical approach of Christianity. So I
would be helped by any comments or thoughts that a person of
your eminence would have to say about Christianity as you see it,
or what you think the Buddha's message, particularly in its Zen
form, has to offer Christianity.

K.S.:   Your friend Mrs. Mitchell from Boston kindly sent your
book [*Zen Catholicism*]. Some pages that I turn over are very
interesting, and I am much impressed. You have a profound
understanding. About your founder, Benedictus: his belief, his
way of life as you have described it, is impressive in comparison
with the monastic life. The short phrase "only God" was inter-

esting to me. To live only with God is the spirit of the monastic life. From this short phrase I seem to understand the full personality and background of your founder.

A.G.: I think that's very interesting, and true to the situation, because Benedict, in his own way, chose a middle path in monasticism. Up to his time, the way of monks was to go off into the desert and to live an extremely austere life of a rather competitive kind. They'd go out in the Egyptian desert and live on three figs a day. Then some other monk half a mile away would learn about this, so he would cut down his diet and live on two figs a day. You see? That kind of competitive asceticism and living by themselves, eremitical lives. On the other hand, there were monks who wanted to live the monastic life but they would go from monastery to monastery to find out which was the most comfortable and easy, and they'd stay as long as they could, until they were thrown out. So Saint Benedict thought the monastic life should be somewhere in between those two extremes, a life of well-ordered service to God and man. Saint Benedict, as I mentioned in that little essay, was concerned with the service of God only, in terms of the ultimate, the Supreme Being. And that worked itself out in the service of man also. Through the history of Western Europe, of course, the Benedictine monks played a very big part. It is sometimes said in the West that Christian monasticism, when it has been at its best, has always been a creative social force everywhere. Has that been as true in the history of Buddhist monasticism, would you say? In the West one hears Buddhism criticized, or, what is reckoned to be its limitation, spoken of as an incomplete social reference. Do you think that the Buddhist monks should be concerned with education or with social work, or would you say the monastic life is essentially a withdrawal and meditation and it belongs to others to help the world along its way?

K.S.: This is a very difficult, fundamental problem, which both Buddhist and Christian monastic life may confront. I think the monastic life should withdraw completely from social activities —not be mixed. And then when a person needs to come out, he should come out positively and engage in social activities. According to your Benedictine rule, a person who lives in a monastery should throughout his life be in a monastery, not come out. Yes, when it is determined in this way, a person should be in the monastery all the time, so as not to split his mind in two. Some other person may engage in so-called worldly activities. There are not so many people in monasteries, even in your country, I think. This is an example of the purely religious life; this is the fountainhead. The fountainhead should not be muddied by many people's steps; it must be kept pure. Then the streams that come from the fountainhead may be drunk by other people. So this narrow, small fountainhead is a place nobody can approach. This is my idea.

A.G.: I think that is very persuasive and consistent. It limits the monastic life to a relatively few people, who are adjusted to that kind of life. In the history of Western Christian monasticism a whole lot of people were involved who were not suited to that intensive form of concentrated meditation—being just the fountainhead.

K.S.: The fountainhead today is a very strong power, which does not have even a small place in which it will not be trodden upon by other people. They want to rush into the place, even though it is a holy place, a sacred place. They want to take pictures and all that, you know. I think this so-called worldly wave may attack the monastic life. Even the consciousnesses of the people in the monastery may reflect this wave, through reading or communication. I can imagine the outlook of some monks from my own experience of more than ten years. When I was in the monastery, my mind was longing for the street; and whenever I came into the street, I always wanted to go back to the monastery.

A.G.: There is a famous saying in a Christian classic, *The Imitation of Christ*, which is about the monastic life: "Whenever I went out among men, I always returned less a man."

K.S.: This was my personal experience. Later I didn't feel that way.

A.G.: What would you feel about those who are at the fountainhead, the meditative spirits who are drawn to that, whose karma leads them to that? What would be the effect upon sentient beings generally, apart from their own centers of consciousness? Would there be some beneficent effect elsewhere from their activities?

K.S.: The fountainhead also is connected with a long flow of water. The deeper the fountainhead, the deeper the water will flow, even if nobody knows where the fountainhead is. Therefore, it is preferable for the fountainhead not to be known. Do you think this is ridiculous?

A.G.: No, not at all. I think it is a suggestive comparison.

K.S.: It is contradictory to the modern sense of society. We never concentrate on going against the modern social sense.

A.G.: Mustn't we in some way accept the fact that the modern world, or what it expresses, has its own value, and that modern people, particularly the younger generation, have their own values, which must be acknowledged, perhaps even supported? Wouldn't you say that the Buddhist faith and the Christian faith must be presented in such a way as to make an impact, make an appeal to the moderns, the younger generation today?

K.S.: I only mean to compare the monastic life to the fountainhead. This stream is not cut off from other social relationships, and this secluded life is influential on the social life outside in a way that positive social activity, which may appeal instantaneously, is not consonant with. Even a century later, even after such a long period of time, I feel the appeal of Benedictus. This appeals to me directly, even through the pages of your book. This is the way it must be kept pure. We are so sensitive to the instantaneous reactions from modern societies. People are very quick to appeal to modern life. But we must not hasten so. This is a timeless influence.

A.G.: Is it possible to combine that deep concern for the preservation of authentic monasticism, the very fountainhead, with a concern for and an interest in circles outside that?

K.S.: This fountainhead should have a surrounding where Christian or Buddhist monk or priest is living. This kind of person can

D

enter the fountainhead freely or go out to the society. Those who have the responsibility to engage in social work are these. There is another group, too, which has no name, either Christian or Buddhist; this is very wide. And at the outside part there is the so-called irreligious person. These are the ones who in later times may be influenced from the inside.

A.G.: From the point of view of the actual history of Buddhism, Sakyamuni's message, is it true that he was in the first instance concerned with the monastic order only, and that King Asoka sustained this and built many monasteries over India and other parts, but that when he died, and his patronage was no longer available, Buddhism spread outside the monasteries, and that was partly responsible for the development of the Mahayana? Does that correspond roughly to the historical facts?

K.S.: I wasn't conscious of this Mahayana and Hinayana relationship at the time of Sakyamuni. But it may relate, as you say, later on.

A.G.: I have been a Benedictine monk now for thirty-seven years, but I am more interested in Christianity than I am in monasticism, and I am more interested in humanity than I am in Christianity. That is to say, I think there are some people, dedicated monastic spirits, who just live in and for the monastic life. There's a Christian saying that a person could be a perfect monk without being a perfect Christian or even a good Christian; and that seems to me a paradox. So that although I wouldn't be other than a Benedictine, and owe a great deal, everything, to that training and background, my own intellectual and theological education has extended my outlook, and I'm interested now in the welfare of ordinary people, of people around—younger-generation people and the hippies. I would like at the end of this journey of mine to say something or write something not particularly for monks, not particularly to sustain the monastic life. While I'm sure that should be somebody's concern, for me it would be a limiting interest. I'd be more concerned to talk to ordinary people.

K.S.: This is my point: the monastic life in Buddhism does not necessarily have to be kept up throughout life. So we understand the monastic life to be the fountainhead life until we see the god and until we are able to live with the god. We have to have confidence that at no time will we miss the god, even in the trifling events of daily life. Then we are able to come out from the monastic life and serve, not the god, but the people. This is the way we understand the monastic life and its value.

A.G.: I think that may be one of the insights that Christianity, Catholicism, and, particularly, monasticism is in need of.

K.S.: Here is the fundamental difference in the structure of Christian and Buddhist thought. Buddhist thought, particularly as represented by Zen, has no image of God in mind. The term is very difficult to discuss, but this is the fundamental point that is different from your situation. But I feel that if we don't talk, both situations are the same. At the moment we talk we differentiate. So if we meet in silence, you and I, the situation is the same, and we understand much better than we would by talking. But when we discuss, we have differences, one of which is that in Zen we have no image of God. Instead, we very freely serve the person, our fellow being.

A.G.: The Catholic theologian or even the sophisticated Catholic would say that Catholicism doesn't have any image of God either.

K.S.: Image includes notion, too, not graphic or so-called image.

A.G.: Well, Thomas Aquinas, for instance, would say that we can have no adequate concept, no notion, of what God is. And he said that it is better to speak about what God is not—very *emptiness*, you might say—than to say anything positive about him. He tried to conceptualize a good deal of Christian doctrine, but then when he reached what seems to have been his own Enlightenment, he said that all he had written seemed like so much straw compared to that.

K.S.: It must be.

A.G.: So that again, isn't there a parallel? I've heard it said that the worship of Amida is hardly distinguishable from popular Christianity. I don't know whether that's true or not. But the

Catholic mystical theologian is very aware of the absolute hiddenness, unknownness of God. It may be true that as long as we are silent we agree. . . . But I was interested in the point about monasticism and its being a temporary affair. My own experience of the Christian monastic life in the West makes me think that that might be a very good thing for Catholicism to adopt. I think that the reason why the Catholic Church has made monasteries permanent has been to some extent a matter of economic convenience—keeping a big institution going with a fixed personnel. That wasn't Saint Benedict's idea in the first place, although he believed in life-long monasticism for the truly dedicated. He was so alienated by the evils of Roman society, as were a lot of other people, that he wanted to found a way of life away from all that. But once the Benedictine monks were able to civilize Europe, in large measure, and make the life of the people more virtuous, then the need for monks to stay all the time in their monasteries, and the urge to do so, was less. And it might have been better if a good many of them hadn't stayed. The younger generation in America now, for instance, has the same desire to dedicate itself, but not to a lifetime commitment. For instance, the Peace Corps has been taking a lot of people away from the religious life. They're there for just three years; it's not a lifetime of service. So I hold no particular case or brief for a lifetime monastic commitment. It just happens to have suited a person like myself. I think the people who are meant for that are relatively few.

K.S.: From my own experience in the monastery this makes sense.

A.G.: There's a question I've been wanting to ask—it has nothing to do with the comparison of Christianity and Buddhism, but with a comparison within the Buddhist, and indeed the Zen, tradition itself. Is it possible to outline briefly the difference between the Rinzai and the Soto emphasis in Zen?

K.S.: To begin with, Soto Zen is a difficult term. What is Soto Zen? I myself don't know very well what it is. At the moment, people understand it as the name attached to Japanese Zen Buddhism after Dogen, the founder, after Eihei-ji began. If that is so, there are great differences between Rinzai and Soto. But if Soto Zen includes the real founders of Soto in the Tang dynasty, Sozan and Tozan, who were the two representative Zen Masters in this dynasty, there is less difference. If it includes the whole Soto history, then Soto after Dogen is a particular modification. Zen was modified to make it suitable to farmers and fishermen, supposed not learned enough to understand the difficult terms. That part of Zen was just cut off; the unlearned were allowed to achieve direct peace of mind through sitting, without any inner illuminations. These inner illuminations may be necessary finally, but there is no time to give them to so-called unlearned persons. It is not necessary to give them difficult problems: they have a problem already. Then they sit silent. This difference comes from Upaya, the method of compassion for the people.

A.G.: What does the word "Soto" mean exactly?

K.S.: "Soto" is the abbreviation of the names of the two patriarchs, Sozan and Tozan. This is the superficial difference. If I touch on a more inner difference, it is very interesting. Rinzai Zen and Soto Zen are two schools of Zen. But in the beginning there were five different schools: Isan, Ummon, Hogen, Rinzai, Soto—with different tinges or colors in the way a Zen Master comes in contact with the ordinary people, not a basic difference. But the deep difference between Soto and Rinzai is that Rinzai Zen takes the position that Enlightenment needs our discipline. Buddhism is a religion which teaches that a human being is originally Buddha, originally immaculate, originally complete in nature. But by the clouds of delusion this moon of completeness . . .

A.G.: The original face.

K.S.: The original face is covered. So we human beings should wipe off this cloud, this stain. This is a common Rinzai Buddhist attitude. Soto Zen takes a different attitude toward the original face: there is no need to wipe off a cloud; there is no cloud. It is our delusion that we have a cloud. Where is the cloud? Our passions are a cloud—but there is no being who has no passions; our desire—but there is nobody without desires. The nature of desires is different but desire itself is original. This is the Soto attitude. In order to wipe off the cloud, we Rinzai use the word or action. This is the Rinzai attitude: I take up this fan. What do you call this? People say, "This is a fan." "No, it is not a fan. What do you say it is?" In such a way we begin, in order to cut into the originality of this fan. So we suffer: this must be a fan; yet the Master says this is not a fan. What should I say? This is the content of meditation. And day and night this simple problem cannot be solved. So we sit and sit and just become one with the fan. Then the problem is understood thoroughly, and that's the moment we get back to the original face.

A.G.: That's the koan. . . .

K.S.: This is a koan, one of the koans. This is a living koan. This is the way Rinzai tries to wipe off the cloud—with some *chance* of initiation, by some means between master and disciple, the experienced one saturated by the light of Dharma and the one who also has a light of Dharma but which light at the moment is covered. This light should break the cloud and illuminate. This is the teacher-and-disciple encounter as used by Rinzai. Soto has no time to use words like this. Fishermen have no time to listen to such words; they have to work from morning till evening. So the master says, "Sit when you come home at night. Sit, sit."

A.G.: Without any koan.

K.S.: Yes. But someone may have the koan by himself. For instance, a farmer becomes old and very uneasy. "I have to die—what shall I do? My heart is not rested. What is the life after my death?" Then he may have a discussion with the teacher. In Rinzai Zen there are interesting questions and answers.

A.G.: Does either tradition of Zen make the distinction between so-called self-power and other power? Do they look for help in solving these problems outside themselves?

K.S.: We do not classify these two. Soto Zen appears to be a little bit other-power-like. But the fundamental attitude is different.

A.G.: The Soto Zen believers or adherents—do they engage in worship of the Buddha?

K.S.: No. When Zen believers worship any image, they become

the worship itself. This is the difference. When they worship, they worship only. They do not worship *some other* object. For the sake of means, there is an object you know. But when they bow their heads toward the image, they become one with the object. Therefore there is no object.

A.G.: It's a kind of identifying with the Dharma in some way, is that right?

K.S.: Well, "identify" is the maximal word in English, I think. But "identify" is still insufficient.

S.K.: I think Dr. Suzuki often used the words "pure action."

K.S.: The word "identification" still has implication. There is no object, still it has a tinge of an unforeseen object in the term itself: "engaged to," "confrontation with." Some Catholic priest who is a very interesting writer has a good article in Dr. Suzuki's memorial issue. He understands Zen in comparison with Catholicism in this way: confrontation with the ultimate being by words and love in Christianity; in Buddhism or Zen, confrontation with ultimate void. I think he comes to understand Buddhism very well, but still this is the nature of words; Western words have this tinge. "Confrontation"—I don't know the etymology, but anyhow "con" has the sense of "two," no?

A.G.: Yes, two fronts, two faces . . .

K.S.: Yes—these two faces see each other, meet. But we have no confrontations. This is a. theological problem. So, acting is acting. Absolute acting—or "great acting," Dr. Suzuki interprets. So when we act, there is nothing to be confronted. Before that act there seem to be certain things it is necessary to confront. For instance, this boy who brought the tea just now is my disciple. When he was in elementary school, he once came to my temple and asked me: "I heard that Zen Buddhism has no image to be worshiped. But in your temple there is a big image. What does it mean?" I was struck by such a question from a little boy. I had no way to answer. I said, yes, it is as you say, but you may learn while you worship that you yourself become the Buddha itself. But for the time being you may not understand what Buddha is. So for this period this Buddha image is necessary. When you come to understand what the real Buddha is, you bow to the Buddha image at that time, too. But the meaning would have become greatly changed.

s.k.:   And that is the real bowing.

k.s.:   Still, we bow before the image, but the meaning, or so-called act itself, is "pure" or "great act," I think.

a.g.:   Does the Buddhist Enlightenment, or Satori, bring with it complete certitude or an unwavering position?

k.s: "Certitude"?

a.g.:   To eliminate all doubt, so that one never is puzzled.

k.s: This is usually supposed to be, because "*prajna paramita*" means "perfect wisdom." But one puzzling problem remains: this is what to do with those persons who still do not realize their own nature. This is a great puzzlement and suffering for a Buddhist. Other than this, there are things that cannot be understood, but one's original heart will not be disturbed by this uncertainty. This much I think we can find in our nature. This is my own interpretation; others may think otherwise. I have no way to disclose my condition of heart, but this is not a problem of understanding; it is a physical situation confronting difficulties. We sometimes hesitate, sometimes do not understand. Or, rather, we should say that everything in the world is difficult, not to be understood, even a little bit. But this difficulty is different from the difficulty before I was initiated into Buddhism. Then my heart itself was shocked or pierced by this uncertainty or doubt. After the initiations, however, there is a difference: in difficulties one has an undisturbed state of mind. I may be shocked when the doctor says, "You have cancer; you may die in a month." I shall be shocked, and maybe my face will grow pale, but I shall hasten to prepare for my death—I have a lot of things to clear up before my death.

a.g.:   So the Buddhist canonical saying "The enlightened man has no likes or dislikes" is a signpost to the way it should be rather than the way it is, is that right?

k.s.:   When I dislike something or some ideology, I dislike it as a "great act." When I like it, I like it as a "great act."

A.G.: So that there is no ego involved. It's a kind of process.

K.S.: It may be interpreted that way.

A.G.: When a disciple of yours has achieved Enlightenment, can you be quite certain?

S.K.: He knows.

K.S.: This is a moment I'm longing for—the young generations to reach that moment. I have had very bitter experience in that— "bitter" means long and involving my personal nature and incapabilities. It took me a long, long, bitter life. You know, other, clever, ones do not stay on that course so long. But I was a scattered person, engaging in a little bit of reading, also engaging in illness—you know, this is also an engagement—and sometimes taken up in military life. Enlightenment cannot be achieved with shallow determination; it needs a very strong will. So it is with anxiety that I look after my young boys, and I hope they will overcome these difficulties.

A.G.: Well, it has been a wonderful interview . . . a wonderful audience! Perhaps I've had as much as I can assimilate for the time being.

Visit of Dom Aelred Graham to Morimoto Roshi at Nagaoka Zen-juku in Kyoto, September 3, 1967.

Sumiko Kudo translated.

A.G.:   This is my first visit to Japan. I've longed for many years to come here to make some study of Buddhism. Even when I was living in America, or in England, where I was brought up, I was interested in Buddhism along with my Catholic theological studies. So I got interested in an amateur sort of way in Zen. According to my understanding, it is the very heart of Buddhism, the essence of the message, and I think that Zen insight has a lot to give to Western Christianity.

M.R.:   I thought that really to understand writing like yours, written by a Catholic or a Christian, I should first read the Bible and other Christian writings. . . . When I was young and first started to make my Zen studies at a monastery, that monastery naturally belonged to a Zen head temple. The founder of that temple, National Teacher Muso, left instructions not only for all his direct disciples, but also for disciples years later. He mentioned two kinds of students who would wish to come to study Zen. First, there are those who straightforwardly cast away everything and concentrate all of themselves on the study of clarifying their true selves. The second group is of those who are not aware of the true self at all, but are attracted by outside surroundings.

These are called the outsiders. Before I even entered the university, I was rather philosophically inclined. I was much interested in Western philosophy, too. In those days all we could study was superficial knowledge of Western philosophy. But I thought that if I was going to deepen my studies, I ought to study Greek and Latin philosophy, and Hebrew, too, and the teachings of Jesus, and I had to come down to Hegel, I thought. I was physically rather delicate, so when I was well enough, my philosophical curiosity was so intense that I tried to do all these studies. But when I got sick, I had to come directly to the point—that is, to clarify the true self. So I threw out all the philosophical, academic, or scholastic studies, and I started to devote myself to the study of Zen. Because I have no background of Western thinking, when some Westerner comes and asks me questions, I don't know how to answer in accordance with a Westerner's knowledge.

A.G.: Well, I want to try to raise some questions that don't require philosophical knowledge.

M.R.: But it can't be helped anyway. Even though a Westerner says that he will ask a question not depending on Western background, still he's a Westerner, so there are some Western elements involved there already.

A.G.: Inevitable, to some extent. The classification Muso Roshi drew, which is very illuminating—is that born of his own experience, or is that a traditional division of the Buddhist?

S.K.: It was left by the founder of the temple where he studied.

A.G.: I see. Because there's a parallel division in Christian spirituality.

M.R.: I would like to be like this myself [He pointed to a reproduction of Giotto's "Sermon of St. Francis to the birds."] If one really has Zen, if he is really Zen itself, he has to work out like that. He may not necessarily have to take the shape or form of a beggar, but he should in some form naturally work out like that.

A.G.: The Christian classification is this: first of all, the disciple starts in the purgative way—that means purification, getting rid of obvious faults and deficiencies. Then he moves to the illuminative way, the way toward Enlightenment, and that's the second stage. The third stage is the unitive way, when the disciple becomes, as it were, one with the Divine, with God. That's a very famous and much used classification in Christian spirituality, which has some parallels.

M.R.: But of classification Muso says that if one is going to be a Zen disciple at all he has to be of the first class. Then all the second- or third-class elements can be erased.

A.G.: How is it discovered by a Roshi or Zen teacher what class you belong to?

M.R.: Since the master and the disciples are living together, by watching a disciple's life it can be easily found out. Some may be very fond of reading books, showing how interested they are in the cultural or artistic development of Zen, because Zen was very closely connected with the culture of China and Japan and the yin-and-yang philosophy of China. If his Zen study is inclined in that direction, it's not the pure Zen at all. If one has attained Enlightenment, only then can all this knowledge be made good use of.

A.G.: Well, what *is* the pure point of Zen studies?

M.R.: To realize one's true self, to be awakened, to search after the true self. It's a kind of prayer—not in the sense of a prayer from which you would expect some help from the outside. It's the searching after the truth.

A.G.: Would you hold that there are members of the first class who could be living in the world as lay people and getting married and conducting business affairs—could they be of the first class, absolutely top-flight Zen people?

M.R.: No. It's impossible.

A.G.: It's not possible?

M.R.: Muso addressed the disciples who came to his monastery for studies. The lay people were not taken into his consideration at all. He was a Zen Master and he addressed his Zen monks.

A.G.: So that Zen is really a very selective, very specialized . . .

M.R.: Yes. There is a belief in Bodhisattvas and Buddhas. And for the lay people who cannot come for concentrated studies, instructions may be given to lead them to faith in Bodhisattvas or Buddhas. . . .

A.G.: Wouldn't this view of the matter—that it is for an elite, a chosen few—lead the enlightened person to feel that he was, as it were, holier than thou, marked off from the others? And he would have his own form of dualistic thinking then.

M.R.: No. If he is marked off, he cannot be an enlightened one. Since the enlightened one is a human being, he has his limitations in all respects. If he comes to realize these limitations, he will come to his own desire to save people in his own way, to tread the way of Zen training together with others. His training is now how to save others. And that training would continue endlessly. There is a Buddhist vow everybody knows: "I vow that I will save innumerable beings, all the beings in the world." At the beginning it just exists as a saying. But when it comes to his own wish, he has to live with it. It's his training now.

A.G.: Well, wouldn't it be wiser, theoretically, to say that according to an individual Roshi's experience, the true Zen path is for the few because he has seen only a few people following it? But he cannot say dogmatically that it's only for the few, can he? Couldn't he be able to say everybody potentially can be a fully enlightened Buddha, and therefore it is better to be less dogmatic about it being just for the few?

M.R.: Both statements are equally true. The first-class disciple may go through all the difficulties and come to his personal Enlightenment. He won't have any problems of his own any longer; they are all solved. But there are many beings around him, and all these people still have all their problems with them, and now all problems are his own. He is enlarged to cover everybody else, or everybody comes into his own being. There is no distinction between I and the others. In a narrow sense he can be called a Buddha because he is enlightened himself. But he has all the problems of all the other people as his own. So unless there is no person suffering in the world, he cannot be called a Buddha.

A.G.: So he's a Bodhisattva then perhaps?

M.R.: Yes. Dogen, the founder of Soto at Eihei-ji, the great Zen

Master in Japan whom no one does not admire, said that Sakyamuni himself and the twenty-one patriarchs in India between
him and Bodhidharma and the six patriarchs who came from
China—none of them, he declared, can be called Buddha. That
is exactly what I am telling you. Including Sakyamuni Buddha
and the twenty-eight patriarchs in India and in China, there are
no Buddhas. This is not my invention, but I am not imitating
Dogen, who said this. It is my own declaration. Recently I found
out that Dogen said the same thing. This is how I came across
this remark by Dogen: At present in Japan there are many in-
stances of suicide. The ratio is very high especially at the University of Kyoto. There are many students here studying Zen and
going to Kyoto University.

A.G.:   In this Zen center?

M.R.:   Yes. In contrast to years ago, when there were only so-called
elites going to the university, recently the situation has changed.
The carpenter's son used to be satisfied to be a carpenter. Now
the carpenter wants to send his son to the university. The sons
may get into some university, but the family culture is not high
enough to sustain them. Japan is a small and still rather poor
country. One has to try very hard to get into a good university if
he is going to get a good job and if he is going to have a good
bride later. There are many who are not able to go through this
successfully, and, as a result, there are many who commit suicide.
There was a student living here—he was the son of a farmer.
While he was here he was a good student, and he was a good
student at the university, too. But when his graduation time
approached, he had to submit his dissertation. When he came
here, there was the understanding that he, together with the
other students, would devote many hours a day to Zazen. But if
he did that, he would not be able to finish his dissertation. To
write his dissertation was not such an easy thing—he still had all
the background study to do. So finally he committed suicide.
Now I have come to think that there is a necessity to teach students that they shouldn't commit suicide. There is a Buddhist
commandment not to kill. Buddha taught that one must not kill

an insect, not a single tiny living creature. Then killing oneself is a sin. With the changes in Japanese life, people have lost touch with the tradition. Now there is a necessity to clarify the relationship between the Buddhist precepts and Zen training itself. Soto people, quoting from Dogen's *Shobo Genzo*, made a small book about the relationship. I wanted to clarify the meaning of this book, and that is how I came across this saying of Dogen's.

A.G.: There's another aspect that I wonder if you could throw some light on: the reconciling of the apparent contradiction between the Buddhist position that, as Sakyamuni taught, one must be "a lamp unto oneself," with the Buddhist position, particularly in Amida Buddhism, and also to some extent in Soto Zen, on worship, perhaps even a cultus of some kind. That would imply, it seems to me, a worship of something other than self, a distinction between the self and something.

M.R.: It is not a contradiction at all for a Buddhist.

A.G.: But I said "an apparent contradiction." Perhaps you could show how it's not a contradiction.

M.R.: At first I myself thought it was a contradiction.

A.G: There you are. I am only a beginner.

M.R.: As I told you, when I was young I wanted to become a Zen monk. But because I was not healthy enough I couldn't make up my mind to become one. In Kyoto there was a Pure Land temple, where I went to live. Temples do not do any productive work at all, and that kind of life was very unfamiliar to me; I was a businessman's son. Because it was a Pure Land temple, they had rituals, in which all the younger disciples had to take part. They did it because they had to do it as a duty. I didn't have to do this, so they were envious of me. I started to do gardening, cleaning, woodchopping, working in the graveyard, all sorts of manual labor. People began to talk about the university graduate who was doing all sorts of manual work, and they said, "Mr. Morimoto is like a living Buddha." Once in a while the school-master would come to see me. I might be working in the grave-yard, doing the weeding, and he would start to ask me questions about Buddhism, and I would answer him while I cleaned the

.garden. Since he didn't have anything to do, he would start weeding, too, the schoolmaster in his black suit. Then I began to realize that in spite of my reputation, I wasn't really good. In a Pure Land temple they say that if you can recite the Nembutsu, the name of Buddha once, you are saved and all the rest is unnecessary. I realized that what I was doing was all the unnecessary work. So I studied under a Zen Master, and somehow passed the first koan. At the beginning, Zen and Pure Land seemed contradictory, but after I solved the first koan, I realized that Zen and Pure Land are not two separate things. I was studying Zen, but still everything I did, cleaning, sweeping, every act of mine was Nembutsu itself. In the case of religious questions, there is nothing like looking in the dictionary for answers.

There is a Bodhisattva statue called Fudomyo, the work of non-work. After Enlightenment one comes to understand the meaning of this statue. There is another called Vinayaka, religious joy represented in sexual terms. Then comes the Aizen-myo-o, which represents anger and craving. This guardian god represents the purified stage of anger and craving. After this comes the Vairocana Buddha, the big statue in Nara. When the student of Zen reaches this stage he comes to realize that a table or heaven or earth or anything is nothing else but the Buddha himself. In order to talk to all sorts of people, the student of Zen should study social science, physical science, and philosophy if at all possible. But nobody can do it. Even Dr. Suzuki, who lived such a long time and did extraordinary work, couldn't do all of this. But there then comes the statue of Maitreya, the future Buddha. Maitreya embodies all these functions. When one comes to this stage one knows what the Buddha statue with one thousand hands and many eyes and faces means. The central face is the Amitabha. There should be thousands and millions of Buddhas representing the sciences, but there should be the Buddha of heaven, Amitabha. After going through all these stages, one comes to appreciate, to know, what Amitabha is. If one's Zen study does not bring him to know what the Amitabha is, his Zen study is not the true one.

A.G.:   And the Pure Land is here, so to speak, if we only come to realize it.

S.K.:   And when it comes to this point, there is no distinction between Catholic and Buddhist.

M.R.:   No. It's not *that* easy. Hakuin was too quick to come to that conclusion. The Pure Land: because it's here, it's far away. This place is at the same time the Pure Land. If it's the Pure Land itself, then we don't have to say that this is the Pure Land or that it's at once the Pure Land. We don't have to use any predicate like this. Because they are different, we have to say this is it.

A.G.:   I can understand that.

M.R.:   There was no true understanding of Pure Land in the Kamakura period—or in Heian or Nara. Then Rennyo, a kind of saint in the Pure Land sect, said there are just one or two Pure Land followers in one district or area. The same thing can be said in Zen, too. There may be many people who practice Zazen, but that doesn't mean they have true Enlightenment. As far as the Pure Land is concerned, True Pure Land, Jodo Shin-shu, the real spirit may be there.

I have a niece who is a Catholic nun, and I have an aunt who is also a Catholic. I used to stay with her, and every day I used to listen to her praying in the next room. She kept on praying for over an hour. At the first stage of the prayer I thought, Oh, my aunt, what a greedy prayer she makes—greedy wishes and desires she is offering to God in her prayer. But toward the end of an hour there was no purpose, none of her own desires or will or hopes any longer—just the adoration of God. In that case it is not different from Nembutsu, the recitation of Buddha's name.

A.G.:   Well, that is the same as the *Gloria in excelsis*, the great prayer in the Catholic Mass: it's just praise; there is no request.

M.R.:   My aunt was deaf. She used to invite me more and more often to come to see her as my Zen studies increased, and she would make me all sorts of gifts of food. We couldn't exchange any difficult questions or discussion, because she was deaf, yet she wanted to do all sorts of things for me. So I thought that

E

progress in one's Zen studies has to be that way: people around the student should be drawn closer, and there should be real mutual understanding and appreciation in the true sense of the word.

A.G.:   Are there not Buddhist thinkers who hold, who teach, that it is possible for certain individuals to become enlightened without any discipline or training—they just *are?*

S.K.:   They are born like that you mean?

A.G.:   Well, they present that appearance. They have overcome, it seems, dualistic thinking, and they feel an identity, or whatever word you like to use, with everything in the world *without* any long preparation or theory or long severe discipline.

S.K.:   Is this person born like that, or is it given all of a sudden without any process of training?

A.G.:   It may develop in the course of his growth and maturity.

S.K.:   I see. But anyway without any severe training?

A.G.:   Without any severe training, without any koans or anything.

S.K: Do you call it Zen Enlightenment or just enlightened spirituality?

A.G.:   I would say, perhaps better, enlightened spirituality, but *certainly* without distinguishing between you and me or this and that.

M.R.:   Enlightenment is just the beginning. True Zen life starts from there. There may be some occasion like that given to somebody without Zen training. If he can go through the process of Zen life after that, it may fully mature.

A.G.:   Do I understand correctly, the end of Zen training is self-realization, to know the true self?

S.K.:   That's the Enlightenment.

A.G.:   Well, what is the difference between Satori and the goal of Zen training?

M.R.:   The vow to save everybody, the vow that would never be achieved, never be rewarded, never be answered.

A.G.:   I think that Daisetz Suzuki regretted in his later life that in his writings he had given so much prominence to the Satori experience, because that was gotten hold of by students in the West, and particularly by the younger generation, and they were all making for that. That's why a lot of them are getting instant Enlightenment on LSD, because that's what it's all about, they think.

M.R.: My teacher, Master Dokusan, used to say that whenever a lay person came to study Zen, he would say to him or her, "You have the mark of sickness on your forehead"—meaning crazy. I may be. But that is not what Zen aims at. It aims at living like that without talking about it or pretending to know about the Enlightenment. If the disciple fails to do that, and starts to talk intelligently about it, that is "big laughter" or "hearty laughter" —he is just to be laughed at. As you see, facing each other from opposite walls in this room are the painting by Giotto of Saint Francis preaching to the birds and a scroll with calligraphy. The Chinese characters represent just the opposite of the painting: "Big laughter." The Zen Master Rinzai has too much philosophical or intellectual flavor, in my opinion. Joshu, a Chinese master who started the koan Mu is much closer to Saint Francis. Kitaro Nishida, who is a famous philosopher of the Meiji period, Dr. Suzuki, and another Nishida, who started Ittoen, the community where everybody works, all manifest the one aspect of Zen life represented by Saint Francis. They are the same. That's about all I have to say.

A.G.: Yes. Well that's all it would make any sense to ask.

M.R.: One Zen Master said, "I should like to take all the Zen Masters in their ceremonial robes in Japan today and drive them all to Ittoen, where everybody works."

S.K.: He wants me to tell that to Shibayama Roshi.

M.R.: When I think of Christian God, the strict side, where no unrighteousness should be allowed, would never come into my notion; just the compassionate Bodhisattva is accepted by me. This is perhaps oriental mentality or tradition.

A.G.: You mean, then, by God a reality that includes both good and evil, is that right?

M.R.: Yes.

A.G.:   Very good.

M.R.:   In other words, the true understanding of Amitabha, the Pure Land Buddha, may lead me closer to Catholic understanding, if I am correct. I spoke of that to Dr. Inge Bretsen, an American, or Swedish-American, who visited here. He agreed and invited me to the States.

My standpoint on the Pure Land is based on the meaning of the seventeenth vow: "Unless everybody in the world attains Buddhahood I would not attain Buddahood myself." That means every Buddha adores the Amitabha Buddha. There are forty-eight vows in Buddhism, but the central vow or prayer is the seventeenth. Whenever I sign my name, I sign it as "Seventeen Old Boy." "Seventeen" I take from the seventeenth vow. "Old" means I'm pretty old. "Boy" means my Zen life is endless; just as for a boy who has started on the journey, it's going to be endless. As a Zen Master I have to listen to the Dokusan of all the students. Because I talk so much of Nembutsu, or recitation of Buddha's name, some of the students may come into my room reciting Buddha's name. I will always say no, because it's just imitation. If they are studying Zen at all, it cannot be meaningful Nembutsu; it's mistaken on that point already. As students, they have not reached the level of saying real Nembutsu yet. They are just imitating. It's like a young girl talking about a love affair. So, because I have to be compassionate, I listen to their Dokusan, but I cannot help feeling that I am engaging in a game of toy soldiers, playing at military affairs.

A.G.:   Like the Catholic story, an apocryphal story, of a little girl four years of age who consecrated her virginity to God, without, of course, knowing what she was doing.

S.K.:   And what did she call herself? Is it just a story?

A.G.:   Well, it's the story of Little Nelley of Holy God—and she couldn't pronounce God; she could just lisp Dod: Little Nelley of Holy Dod.

Conversation between Gary Snyder
and Dom Aelred Graham at the Snyders' home
in Kyoto, September 4, 1967.

Irmgard Schloegel and Dana Fraser were also present.

G.S.: Irmgard and I were both disciples of Oda Sesso Roshi, who died a year ago. Now we're in the position of choosing what to do next. On the sixteenth and seventeenth there will be the first-year ceremony of his death, which we will attend. Then it is proper for us to take a new Roshi if we wish. Well now, tell us, how do you come to be here?

A.G.: I've had many interviews, and nobody's asked me that question. I had a long interview this afternoon with somebody described as the most outstanding Christian in Japan—we won't name him. I asked him to tell us about Christianity in Japan. He said that he didn't know very much about that, but that he would tell us about his own Christianity. So we got his life story.

H.T.: It took over half an hour.

A.G.: You're the first who's been kind enough to ask me what my project is, giving me the chance to ventilate my illusory ego. I finished my job as prior of the Benedictine Priory at Portsmouth, which was very worthwhile and congenial, but rather tiresome, because administrative work is not quite my line.

G.S.: How long did you do that?

A.G.: For sixteen years.

G.S.: And the job was essentially administrative?

A.G.: Well, no, it wasn't, because there was so much pleasant co-operation and so many people I could delegate things to that I had time for other things, too, and was able to do a little bit of writing. I always had an interest in Eastern religions, particularly Buddhism. I noticed that thirty years ago in my theological notes there were parallel passages from Buddhist scriptures and authorities. I wrote a little essay on the possibilities of links or insights between Zen and Orthodox Christianity. I wanted to call it *Zen Catholicism?*, but the publisher insisted that the title would be stronger if I just called it *Zen Catholicism*. Anyhow, that had a moderate success—it's now in paperback, in German and French. Now I realize I'm a bit ashamed of parts of it, but perhaps most of it can stand up. So I told the publisher I would like at the end of my term of office to study Buddhism on the spot, see the Mahayana in Japan, go on to the Theravada, perhaps in Thailand, Ceylon, and Burma, if one can get into it, then Hinduism in India, then Islam, going farther west. He said that he was interested.

The church at present is in rather poor shape, and I don't think that the Second Vatican Council has done very much more than open a few windows, as Pope John suggested. But the really radical problems of what religion is all about have not been discussed, and *cannot* be discussed at the organizational level. I would hope to go back to the West and work out something in terms of what religion really is, and let some of the Buddhist, particularly Zen, insight into Catholicism. Catholicism still is pretty hung up on verbal formulae and credal statements. While those have their value, I want to indicate that they have to be seen through, as the great theologians saw long ago. I want to elaborate that, but I want to be able to do it not only at the more or less high-powered scholarly and theological level, but also at the level of our contemporaries. That's why I think an encounter like this, with you, could be of equal value with an official encounter with Japanese Catholicism, or possibly with the Roshis. I met a hippie in San Francisco who said, "If only somebody could write a book that could say the sort of things you could say to people of your generation and also could speak to my background." I don't want to be one of the boys; there's nothing more fatal for an old stager like me. But I feel it's possible to get on that wave length and say something to the younger generation, who may be the salt of the earth. Harold regards himself as an old stager, too.

H.T.:   Not only that, but I'm profoundly bourgeois. I have nothing to do with anything hippie at all.

G.S.:   I find myself in a funny position, being at that age when I can talk to both elders and younger people equally.

H.T.:   The term "spokesman" is applied to you and Allen Ginsberg.

A.G.:   Yes, you're the spokesmen for the hippies.

G.S.:   There's a whole world of discussion right there about what the younger generation is up to and the kind of spiritual seeking and consciousness that's being manifested. That's a whole world with its own politics, so to speak. It's very different from the spiritual politics of the beat generation. The present phenomenon was rather unpredictable. There's nothing new about alienated youth forming its own society outside the established social order; it started from the beat generation. What we didn't predict was sheer number. Some of the music that's being played now wasn't predictable either—the fusion of baroque and jazz and Negro blues and Indian music into a whole style of dance music. The new groups and their music were beyond our dreams; we didn't think they would catch on that fast. As Northrop Frye pointed out years ago, the aesthetic orientation is basically oriental. Confucius said, as well as Plato, that as soon as you change the mode of music you change the government, that politics and music are related.

H.T.:   Plato was for kicking all musicians out.

G.S.:   Whereas Confucius was for bringing poets into government and letting them run it. He said that the study of poetry teaches you the names of flowers and trees and animals, then it gives you a proper sense of decorum, and thirdly it trains your character, so that people who know poetry can be good governors.

A.G.: I remember a saying of his related to that that "the business of the governor is to call things by their right name."

G.S.: The ideal in the Confucian government is that when everything is running smoothly, government consists of rites and music—the only important bureau is the bureau of rites.

H.T.: The hippies have a sense of decorum, by the way, which the beats did not.

G.S.: That's because they are not in opposition to an old order. They are convinced that they've won already, that the old order has passed out of existence.

H.T.: It's something you have compassionate hindsight about.

G.S.: They don't have the sense of antagonism, hostility, and paranoia which went through the fifties with an accompanying self-destructiveness, a tendency toward alcoholism or heroin addiction, suicide, and a kind of romantic mystique of self-destruction, so that it was considered tragically beautiful to see someone go down through drug addiction. Now everybody's for eating brown rice and being healthy.

H.T.: Was the beat movement filled with a lot of people who came back from the Second World War?

G.S.: The fathers of it were in the Second World War. They had gone to it or hadn't gone to it, which amounts to the same thing. Like Ginsberg hadn't gone to it because he had pounded on the desk and wept and said he was homosexual or something and got sprung out. But either way it was a traumatic thing for that generation.

A.G.: Well, somebody has to stop people like Lyndon Johnson and traumatic things like the Vietnam war, and it seems that the only people who are doing anything about it are those one meets in San Francisco.

G.S.: Whom did you see there?

A.G.: Did you ever meet a wonderful character called Gavin Arthur?

G.S.: Oh yes. He did my horoscope three times.

A.G.:   Yes, he did mine. He's the grandpapa of the hippies. He said mine was a terrible horoscope.

G.S.:   He calls himself a Jungian astrologer.

A.G.:   It was in Gavin's pad that I met a number of these characters.

G.S.:   Gavin is one of those people who've been right with everything through the years.

A.G.:   You've read his book, *The Circle of Sex?* Whether you're the two o'clock man or the eight o'clock woman. He did Harold's horoscope too.

H.T.:   He said I had nine planets in the House of Confinement—nine out of ten—and that I'd end up either in a monastery or in a penitentiary.

A.G.:   He is quite wonderful because of his original background. He's gone through an awful lot and is mellow and unembittered. He spent four or five years selling newspapers in Union Square in San Francisco. Most of his discussions with Kinsey took place when Kinsey used to come to him at furtive moments while he was selling his newspapers and talk to him on the street corner in San Francisco.

G.S.:   Mrs. Sasaki knew his brother.

A.G.:   Oh yes. He has wonderful stories about the early days of Mrs. Sasaki.

G.S.:   She belonged to an organization called the Tantric Circle, which was run by a man called the Great Om.

A.G.:   Yes, Nyack. Bernard somebody or other. Gavin joined the Ku Klux Klan with the special purpose of doing away with this character.

H.T.:   Have you run into that group?

I.S.:   No, but one picks up a bit of information—and sooner or later everything finds a home in London, even if it's only three or four people.

A.G.:   What about LSD, Gary?

G.S.:   I'm still thinking about it.

A.G.:   All the better: you're not going to make any infallible pronouncements.

G.S.:   Certainly not about the relationship between LSD and mystical experiences or religious practice. I don't suppose either of you has had LSD.

H.T.:   An analyst told me I'd better not.

A.G.:   Two hippies came to me privately in San Francisco and said, "Will you smoke marijuana with us? It's illegal, and you could go to the penitentiary. But we think it would be a great experience for you." So I did smoke for a couple of hours with them. I must confess I felt a little bit high, but it wasn't nearly as stimulating as a Martini.

H.T.:   I smell pot at the moment.

G.S.:   No. That's my pinewood bath.

A.G.:   I've never taken a trip. I would try if I thought those whose opinions were worthwhile having thought it worth doing for a person like myself.

G.S.:   Well, I wouldn't say that taking an LSD trip was necessary or essential for anybody. People like you and like me who are seriously concerned with what's happening in the spiritual life of the young would be well advised probably to know what that experience is. Because certainly nobody has any qualification to talk about it who hasn't tried it.

H.T.:   Have you tried it?

I.S.:   No. That's what I was saying to Gary: I've made up my mind to try it.

G.S.:   To give you an answer about LSD, I should really talk about my practice a little bit. The Tibetans always say, and this is what I would say to you, "Who is your guru and what is your *sadhana?*" This is, "Who is your teacher and what is your practice?" Then you would say you're a Catholic or a Sufi or anything else. My original teacher was the American Indian, and my *sadhana* was going out and living in nature by myself without anything, which I started doing when I was an adolescent.

H.T.:   In what area?

G.S.:   In the Pacific Northwest. My college days were spent in anthropology, which means, in America, concretely, American Indian studies.

A.G.: Marco Pallis said there's a lot to be learned from the American Indian, and Frithjof Schuon says they're the people who have a *tremendous* lot to teach us.

I.S.: And Jung said so, too.

G.S.: This is what I have returned to. This is also one of the most remarkable things about the hippie phenomenon—their relationships and sympathy for the American Indian. My first response to Western thought and Christianity was qualified by my feeling for nature and for the American Indian. I was never able to accept Christianity as a child because the two or three times I went to Sunday school I raised the question about the future of animals and was told that animals didn't have souls. I wasn't able to accept that—on a common-sense practical basis. I felt that living creatures constituted some kind of a community or unity, which was my own natural mystical experience. So I lost interest in religion and spent a lot of time in the woods. I became interested in Buddhism at the end of my college career. It led me to leave graduate school, where I was doing advanced work in anthropology and linguistics. I left it to pursue the Dharma, which had become more interesting to me. That was when I had begun to read Suzuki. But almost at the same time I had my first experience with peyote; it was with Indians. So my spiritual career has been half in the realm of peyote and shamanism, American Indian contacts, nature mysticism, animism, long hair and beads, and the other half concerned with the study of Sanskrit and Chinese and the traditional philosophies of the Orient. These are the things which led me, when I was twenty-six, to come to Japan, live in a temple, and make myself the disciple of a Zen Roshi. I started Zazen before I came to Japan. I taught myself Zazen from books.

A.G.: Same as I did.

G.S.: You get the posture and breathing without too much difficulty just by experimentation. During the three-year period before I came to Japan, when I was doing Zazen, I was also taking peyote from time to time. Peyote was very available during those years.

A.G.: Is that very different from mescalin?

G.S.: Same thing.

A.G.: Aldous Huxley—*Doors of Perception.*

G.S.: This was something we were doing before Huxley or any-body else was writing books about it. I'm talking about 1948. I had just heard of peyote in anthropological studies and read Slotkin's account of Menomini peyotism and became interested. So I have seen peyote. Then mescalin came out, then psilocybin, then LSD. I've tried them all as they appeared. They've been enormously educational for me, but they have always constituted a slightly different stream from my basic interest until recently. They have come to revolve around the same things.

A.G.: Did you experiment with these drugs with supervision of any kind or just on your own?

G.S.: On my own! Who could be the supervisor?

A.G.: But I understand if you take LSD you might want to climb the walls or throw yourself out the window or something.

G.S.: In those days we didn't bother waiting to find out; we just said, "O.K. let's see what it does."

A.G.: Well, that's what Alan Watts says—in any spiritual advance you have to take a risk.

G.S.: Sure. All of the lore used in LSD today, which is being circu-lated in underground newspapers—"If you're going to take a trip do this and don't do that"—it's all based on the gathered experi-ence of all of us over the last fifteen years. It's a kind of body of folklore, kitchen lore, that's grown up about what to do—what to do when you feel bad and how to get out of it and how to get into it and so forth.

A.G.: What I hope to hear from you is what the hippie generation thinks about Christianity.

G.S.: I don't know if they think very much about it.

A.G.: What they don't think then—I mean, why they've passed it up.

G.S.: The Zen strain of thought and the Zen influence—it's a very peculiar thing and it's not strong now in the United States. And it's not strong for exactly the wrong reasons: for a misunderstanding of D. T. Suzuki. I'll go back to your book for a little bit. You are worried in the book about possibilities of antinomianism, moral anarchy, and all that.

A.G.: That was a little bow to the censors.

G.S.: Well, that's a real worry. But it's not a real worry from the Zen influence. That's the curious thing.

H.T.: The reverse.

G.S.: Yes. As a matter of fact, I've never known anybody who did anything particularly irresponsible or justified anything he did whatsoever on the basis of Zen—ever. The danger of Zen is not that people become moral anarchists—it's quite the opposite. It's that they become complete supporters of whatever establishment is around. That is the *real* moral anarchism of Zen. "Morals don't matter, so support the government."

H.T.: Sumiko's attitude toward the hippies in Japan is that they're a bunch of boys and girls who are too stupid to listen to their teachers and parents.

G.S.: Well, there you are. That's the moral anarchism that runs through Chinese and Japanese Buddhism, not just Zen. The danger of antinomianism and anarchy is very slight.

I.S.: In the Japanese field I entirely agree.

G.S.: In America the other side of it is that nobody who smokes pot or does whatever they do needs Zen to justify it. They just do it. So there is a very definite question involved in the problem of Zen. It's the question of how you relate to the society in terms of how you find a moral or ethical commitment which leads you to run counter to the society.

A.G.: That's the question I've been raising. We've been meeting quite a few Zen Roshis. There's an otherworldliness and austerity and asceticism about them that puts the Christian monks, the Trappists and Carthusians, *way* in the shade. They're so withdrawn, so aristocratic—particularly somebody like Kobori San.

G.S.: Kobori San—well he's a seventeenth-century type. He's a seventeenth-century Zen aesthete. He's a lovely man, but his consciousness is in the seventeenth century.

A.G.:   Very remote from the modern world.

G.S.:   In the Christian world, for better or for worse, there is much more serious thought about the modern age and what to do with it than there is in the Buddhist world. The Buddhist world doesn't admit the modern world is anything. However, I'm trying not to talk about Zen in Japan at the same time as talking about the evolution in America—those are two separate subjects. They have no connection at all.

A.G.:   We were told that the younger generation of Japanese didn't think anything of Zen, looking at these characters around here in Kyoto. But when they learn that the Americans and the hippie generation are interested in Zen, they think there must be something in it, and they're beginning to apply themselves.

G.S.:   That's true. It's going to be a feedback.

H.T.:   Caucasian backlash.

G.S.:   In fact, it's already happened to some extent. In Japan there's a genuine spirituality among some of the young people my wife and I know.

Let's go back to the first question, about the use of psychedelics. None of us predicted that the use of psychedelics would expand so and be used so widely. When I say "us" I mean myself and Ginsberg and a few others who knew the psychedelic thing and had experienced it and also had been around places like India and Japan. We didn't think that such numbers of people would take it. And there's no doubt about it that LSD has been a real social catalyst and amounts to a genuine historical unpredictable. It's changing the lives of all kinds of people.

H.T.:   Suzuki Roshi said in New York that the LSD experience was entirely distinct from Zen.

G.S.:   Well, in practice he doesn't prevent anyone from sitting in the Zendo. And he has said privately that people who have started to come to the Zendo from LSD experiences have shown an ability to get into good Zazen very rapidly.

A.G.:   He came out to the ranch I was staying at, and there were two or three hippies there. They sat around listening for a whole evening, and then they talked to me later. The effect on these hippies of ·the description of Tassajara monastery was one of fright; they were scared by the idea of sitting for hour after hour in the Zendo. However, they were quite prepared to smoke marijuana and take occasional trips.

G.S.: It's hard to articulate all this, because I'm still trying to think it out. The thing is that there are all kinds of orders of experiences—mystical, spiritual—there's not just one, and all paths do not lead to the same goal. There's a tremendous variety of possibilities in spiritual practice, and there are realms of the unconscious, the mind, and the spirit. People in the modern world will get into any realm of the inner world suddenly, and will accept that realm as an absolute because it's the first time they've found it.

I.S.: I entirely agree.

G.S.: This is the danger of it: LSD, psilocybin, and all of these psychedelics take you into all kinds of inner realms. For the ordinary person who has no teacher, no kind of training behind him, any one of these realms will present itself with more authenticity than anything he's previously known in ordinary life, unless he's a very remarkable person. So the danger is, in a sense, the danger of Hinduism, that every trip is the end. People who take a number of trips overcome this by discovering that there are all sorts of possibilities, realizing the relativism of it. If they are gifted and sincere and have good karmic roots, they will proceed through their experiences to the end and arrive at a place that is very profound—through the use of LSD alone. I haven't done real LSD practice, which is once a week or even three times a week for several months, but I've known people who've done that.

H.T.: Does it alter the efficiency of the mind?

G.S.: Which mind?

H.T.: Let's say the everyday mind of a secretary in an industrial office—the most awful thing imaginable, but it gets the job done.

G.S.: Oh definitely. It alters that efficiency, to begin with, by removing the interest in doing that kind of work at all.

H.T.:   Zen wouldn't alter that; it might heighten it.

G.S.:   Well, this is Zen's problem.

H.T.:   I'm not convinced.

G.S.:   One thing at a time; we'll come to that next. What LSD and all the psychedelics do is open up many realms of the mind and present one with possibilities of supernatural powers, whatever they are. The LSD world is best understood in the language and mythology of Hinduism and of Vajrayana Buddhism, because, like Vajrayana and certain schools of Shivaism, it proceeds from psychological and supernatural powers, spiritual experiences. Just as Vajrayana leads a person to Enlightenment through the exploitation and development of powers, LSD proceeds in this direction. This is, in Buddhist terms, the Sambhoga-kaya path, the path of the realm of ideal forms and the Bliss body of the Buddha. Zen has proceeded on the Dharma-kaya path, which is the path of emptiness, the path of formlessness. Consequently, in its practice, in working with a Roshi, if you have hallucinations, visions, extraordinary experiences, telepathy, levitation, whatever, and you go to your Roshi, he says, "Pay no attention to it; stick to your koan." So Zen does not explore those realms. Although in the process of Zen studies, koan study, especially in your first koan, when you're doing Zazen for many hours, for many weeks or months, you become aware of these different realms, you block yourself from going into them at all—you are them. You leave those all behind; they're classified as *mozo*, delusions, in the Zen school. Whereas in Shivaite Yoga and in certain schools of Tibetan Buddhism you take each of those realms up one at a time and explore it as part of your knowledge of yourself. Both of these schools of Buddhism, Zen and Tibetan Buddhism, have the same historical roots, the Madhyamika and the Yogacara. They're both schools of practice. Apart from the Paramitayanas, both schools assert that it's possible to become enlightened in one lifetime, and that you do not need to perfect yourself in countless lifetimes. So they're extremely close. They're closer than any other schools in Buddhism. However, one proceeds in Zen by going directly to the ground of consciousness, to the contentless empty mirror of the mind, and then afterward, after ten or fifteen years of koan study, coming up bit by bit, using each of the koans as an exploration of those realms of the mind, having *seen* the ground of the mind first. The other, Tibetan Buddhism, works by the process of ten or fifteen years of going *down* bit by bit, till the ground of consciousness is reached, and then coming up swiftly. So that ultimately they arrive at the same place, but the Zen method is the reverse of the Tibetan.

A.G.: May I interject a point made by Morimoto Roshi yesterday that Enlightenment, Satori, is a beginning, not an end.

G.S.: That's the Zen approach.

A.G.: And that his Zen life goes on and on, that the Bodhisattva's function is to diffuse this Enlightenment to help to save all sentient beings. And he goes on striving to save, to pass on to others something of that Enlightenment.

G.S.: The Bodhisattva's vow is taken equally seriously by all Mahayana schools. What Morimoto Roshi is saying, I think is what I'm saying: the Zen practice is to go to Satori directly. Solving the first koan is "Satori."

A.G.: That's right. This koan is usually Mu, or "the sound of one hand clapping."

G.S.: But that is not the end of Zen life.

A.G.: The Zen life is to lead the life of compassion toward all others.

I.S.: It's not the end of Zen training either.

G.S.: No. That Satori is not the end of Zen training. It's the beginning of Zen training. This is where Suzuki and all the other writers on Zen are misleading. Satori does not end anything, but opens up the world of Zen practice to you. And all the other koans follow on that first Satori. Those other koans, as they accumulate and you work on them all, are the equivalent of all the areas of the mind you have cut through in working back from the bottom. So that you have to see and examine all these things that you have ignored in the process of getting down to that Mu. After that Mu, nothing; you have to come back to all those things that are something. Practicing the Bodhisattva's vow in concrete terms is part of that, but even that comes after you've finished your training and you go out and live in the world as a Zen monk. But, then, the Bodhisattva's vow is an enormous thing in the Mahayana. My first teacher, with whom I was ordained, said to me, "There is no end to practice. Even Sakyamuni Buddha is continuing his practice somewhere. Through however many lives, you're dedicating yourself to this—not just in this lifetime."

A.G.:   What does the statement "The deluding passions, I vow to conquer them" mean? Passions are part of human nature, aren't they? Presumably the operative word is "deluding."

G.S.:   The operative term is "thieves of the mind" in Chinese: "I vow to conquer the thieves of the mind"—those things that steal my mind.

A.G.:   That's excellent: that could be good Thomism.

G.S.:   Those things that pull me away from my concentration, my vow, my practice. So it's a little bit different from "deluding passions."

A.G.:   Do you feel that you can throw any light on this from the Western point of view? Where's your fan, Harold? If you're asked to write a poem or discourse on this ["Form is emptiness"], what would you say?

G.S.:   *Shiki soku ze ku.* It's not the same as *Ku soku ze shiki* ["Emptiness is precisely form"], that's one thing I've learned. "Form is the same as emptiness" and "Emptiness is the same as form" are both phrases from the Prajna Paramita Sutra. Each one moves in a unique direction, which is complementary to the other, but it really moves; it moves way out. When Yamada San took LSD and was sitting up on the rock, he said, "This isn't form is the same as emptiness; this is emptiness is the same as form." He saw the difference. So I would say that "Emptiness is the same as form" is the Dharma-kaya. And "Form is the same as emptiness" is speaking from the Sambhoga-kaya, two aspects of the Trinity of Mahayana philosophy. It's the same as your Trinity.

A.G.: The famous Buddhist Trinity, so far as I understand it, is the Buddha, the Dharma, and the Sangha.

G.S.: That's the three treasures. This is the same as that trinity actually, expressed in philosophical terms. The Dharma-kaya, or Truth body, the Sambhoga-kaya, or Bliss body, and the Nirmana-kaya, or Illusion body. To put it in Brahmanistic terms, the Eternally Unmanifest is the Dharma body; the Divine as Manifested is the Sambhoga-kaya, and the Manifest as Manifest is the Nirmana-kaya. Or, in Buddhist terms, Emptiness, Sunyata, is the Dharma-kaya; the action of all the Bodhisattvas and Buddhas in all their realms with all of their techniques of compassion is the Sambhoga-kaya, the Bliss body, and the historical incarnation of enlightened beings like Gautama is the Nirmana-kaya, the body of Illusion. That leads to another subject. But let me finish what I was saying about acid and all kinds of dope. I don't understand about this stuff really, except that it's there.

A.G.: That's much more reassuring than to tell us that you understand it, Gary.

G.S.: Nobody understands why it works, and it opens up as many questions as it solves, because it's unpredictable and it has different realms of possibilities. For instance, Allen Ginsberg, after going on countless trips, went to India to seek a guru. I met him in India, and we traveled together. The reason he went to India, he said, was that he was exhausted with having so many contradictory absolute realities presented to him. Every time he went on a trip it presented itself as an absolute, and when he added them all up, they were contradictory.

A.G.: But apparently Brahmanism is not fazed by contradictions.

G.S.: Now you're talking philosophically. These are concrete spiritual experiences. The thing that's happening now is that all kinds of people are taking this stuff and are having their minds opened up in many unpredictable directions. There's a statistical probability of one out of about five that somebody who takes this stuff is going to have an experience of blinding light, waves of ecstasy and bliss, is going to see the face of God in the center of the sun or some place like that, and is going to feel commun-

ion and comradeship with all beings and all varieties of existence. Then he's going to say, "College can't teach me anything,
who wants to work, the universe is community and bliss and love
and knowledge, and, whatever comes, I will live by that." So
now they're walking the streets with long hair and beads.

H.T.: Can they express it when they talk to somebody?

G.S.: No. Because it's not verbal. This is a characteristic of the
aesthetic development of the hippies: poetry is not so important
to them. The novel is a dying art form. Music is most important.
You ask me what they think about Christianity. They read
whatever comes into their hands. The religious material that is
most in tune with that experience is Hindu mythology, the
mythology of the Puranas, and the mythologies of the American
Indian. They don't have an interest in Zen. They say to you,
"Man, that Zen stuff, those Zen guys, they don't have any discipline—they just sit around laughing all the time; that's just
words." They say, "Those Zen cats, they don't care—they eat
meat. We care, we don't eat meat."

H.T.: And they eat that dreadful microbiotic diet?

G.S.: Yes, the hippies eat that.

H.T: It's very unhealthy.

G.S.: It's not unhealthy. It's brown rice and vegetables. The hippies in San Francisco put down Zen because they misunderstand
it from Suzuki. They put down Zen for being undisciplined, for
having no practice, for having no morals.

I.S.: Suzuki never stresses it; that's true enough. The word Zazen
hardly appears in Suzuki.

H.T.: Among the people who are kindly looking after us there's a
real reverence for Suzuki.

G.S.: They are lay Zen people.

H.T.: Shibayama Roshi has a real reverence for Suzuki.

G.S.: That could be. But most of the old Zen monastic world, if
they've heard of him at all, regard him as a popularizer. I
wouldn't want to put Suzuki down, because all of us owe so
much to him. In many ways he should have done it in reverse:
he should have written what he wrote in English in Japanese,

and he should have written in English what he wrote in Japanese, because the things he said in English didn't *have* to be said to the Western world. For instance, the *Japanese* have to be told that it's all right to be wild and that it's all right to experience total freedom and break conventions. The Americans don't have to be told that; they'll do it anyway.

A.G.: To some extent *perhaps*, but there's an awful bourgeois puritanical strain running through Americans—even the American younger generation.

G.S.: Well, this is my drawback—I never meet those people in America. I almost can't escape from a society of turned-on people, which amounts to ten or fifteen thousand.

A.G.: It's pretty permissive and will go along with pretty well everything?

G.S.: It's permissive in it's own terms. It has its own values, which are quite strong. The old criticism of beatniks or hippies is that they're not unconventional; they have conventions just like everybody else. But the point is that they are *different* conventions. In matters of style and dress the hippies are much more severe than sloppy middle-class suburbanites, for example. . . . To wind up about marijuana and LSD. They work. They work in all kinds of unpredictable ways, but they really do work.

A.G.: What does marijuana do to one?

G.S.: Marijuana focuses the senses. The sensations it produces are in some curious way spiritual, and also natural. Even in the less profound LSD experiences, everyone reports that they have for the first time seen the clouds, felt the wind, been aware of the birds, that they have had this sense of the living quality of their cat or their dog, the consciousness of the intelligence in the eyes of the animal, that the old ancient powers of earth and sky become real, the *kami!* Now, this is what I'm trying to say: LSD is primitive religion. LSD is *the* basic religion before all the organized religions got started. That's the experience it presents —of natural powers, natural forces. From that and certain other experiences I've had I tend nowadays to look on Buddhism, Christianity, Hinduism, Islam, you name it, as being degenerations that come with complex, civilized social systems that are in themselves not really so good. But then, I've been reading Lévi-Strauss lately, too, and I have a strong bias toward the validity of the primitive culture as opposed to the civilized culture.

A.G.: How much of the experience of awareness of wind, clouds, sky, and so on is really a proportionate human response to those phenomena? How much of it has been jazzed up by an inner stimulation that gives a kind of terrific thrill but really a disproportionate experience of those phenomena, so that you get the impression that the wind and the clouds and so on have a significance in the human scene and general world scene quite out of proportion to their basic significance? The last person I asked that confessed that he was out of his depth there. "I don't follow it," he said.

G.S.: I don't follow it either. How can they be out of proportion? This is where we *live*. This is the world of form that we are in.

A.G.: Well, I'm just a seeker. . . . There's nothing phony about this. I'm not asking any Socratic questions. Is it just as it is when you've had a few Martinis—there's a kind of overstimulation? You see people around with a slightly glazed appearance. They're much more interesting, in a way, and you feel you can get much closer to them and say things to them that you couldn't say otherwise. Now is *that* the real world or is the real world the *non-Martini* world, for instance?

G.S.: Well, there must be a balance.

A.G.: Somewhere between the two. The middle way.

G.S.: Actually, there is no contradiction between normal consciousness and the other. For example, the hippies make good money.

H.T.: The hippies make the money they do because the society is so prosperous that it's fascinated by eccentricity.

G.S.: It's not just eccentricity—they are good musicians.

H.T.: But that's because the society they live in is able to pay for music.

G.S.: Societies have always been able to pay for music. All civilized societies have paid for music. These people practice; they know their craft; they play their instruments well. The problem is that these people in the West are seriously concerned with what is worth the time and what is not, and that's where they're confused. Japanese people will knock themselves out from the crack of dawn till the middle of the night, sweeping, typing, writing letters, riding the train back and forth, reading, sewing, you name it. It's the most accomplishment-oriented culture on the globe. But what are they accomplishing? That's another question. They don't know how to sit down and relax or practice an inner life.

H.T.: Oh they must!

A.G.: They sit hours and hours, all through the night.

G.S.: No. For instance, they can only get Zen across in Japanese culture under the guise of being efficient and businesslike. My trip through India in 1960, which was a pilgrimage to the holy sites of Buddhism, was a great education for me on the other side of spirituality.

A.G.: They know how to relax, do they, in India?

G.S.: And in doing so they are not wasting their time. They know how to sit there, and they're sitting in eternity. This is what Japanese, and perhaps Chinese, culture can't do: it can't sit in the *lalita asana*, the pose of play.

I.S.: Yet, to defend the Japanese, the highest samadhi is the yoga samadhi, and that is play.

G.S.: Well, I don't know anybody who's gotten very good at that —maybe it can't be seen by us.

A.G.: I would guess every nation or locality has to do it according to its own karma.

G.S.: To finish up the question of LSD: it's remarkable and effective, and it works in terms of forms, devotions, personal deities, appearances of Bodhisattvas, Buddhas, and gods to your eyes. It doesn't work in terms of non-forms, emptiness.

A.G.: How does it work in terms of interpersonal relationship? Does it make you more affable, more compassionate, more considerate?

G.S.: It sure does. It makes everybody believe that they should love everybody else. And it's not very ascetic in that orientation, so that it's very Tantric or Shivaite in the nature of the experience.

A.G.: It's a wonderful scene, Kyoto. I must say, from my own background I'm very fascinated by the Zen approach—it strikes me as quintessential. I said to Sumiko, "I see the Dalai Lama is going to set foot in Tokyo in the next few weeks. He's supposed to be the latest incarnation of the Buddha. What do you think about that?" She said, "I don't know him—I've never met him."

G.S.: That's the trouble. That's the trouble with Zen: they don't know anything about Buddhism.

A.G.: We must tell her that tomorrow.

G.S.: My position is that I am a Buddhist, which means that I have respect and reverence for the Dharma as taught by the Buddha. But I recognize that the Buddha Dharma is but one variety of the Sanatana Dharma, the Eternal Dharma. I'm a follower of the Buddha Dharma, the Dharma as taught by successive generations of enlightened human beings, the Dharma as handed down in the human realm, as distinguished from the Hindu Dharma, which is the Dharma as taught by the gods. You can approach that Dharma through LSD, but you can't approach the Buddha Dharma very easily through LSD. As a Buddhist, my practice is Zen, but that's only my practice. Zen is not the end-all, and it doesn't present all the possibilities of the Buddha Dharma by any means. Nor is that necessarily my final practice or my only practice. I also practice certain other kinds of meditation, such as mantra chanting, which belong to other schools of Buddhist meditation.

H.T.: Christianity is a Dharma taught by God—a revealed religion?

G.S.: Christianity from our standpoint is what we call a heaven-and-earth *yana*, a vehicle of heaven and earth.

H.T.: To link the two?

G.S.: Yes.

H.T.: Christians who study Zen make the distinction between the natural and the supernatural order. Zen can teach them contemplation, but their religion, they insist, is revealed.

G.S.: I don't understand that difference between natural and supernatural. That's Dumoulin's position.

H.T.: And Lassalle's.

G.S.: Well, maybe it's true, except that I don't understand what it's about.

H.T.: I don't think it's integral to Christianity.

A.G.: It seems to me that you can only talk about what is basic to Christianity as it has hitherto been expounded. After all, we are still early Christians. Christianity is only two thousand years old, and the world is going to go on for a million years, with a little luck. The distinction between the creator and the creature is regarded by orthodox exponents of Christianity as basic. So on that basis, it seems to me, it's a kind of corollary: the supernatural on the God side, and the natural, which is the creature side of this dual relationship. Within the terms of that framework, or cosmology, it's fairly natural to use those terms. But even within Christianity itself there is an acknowledgment of the fact that man becomes divinized—you get it in the New Testament, in the Second Epistle of Peter, that man is a participator in the Divine Nature. You get the Catholic doctrine of grace worked out in the Greek Fathers and Thomas Aquinas that man shares or participates in some way in the Divine Nature, so that to some extent you get a bridging of the gap. But it is still usual, and in some quarters mandatory, to use the word "supernatural" as against "natural." A certain Jesuit writer, Père de Lubac, wrote a book on the *surnaturel*, in which he tried to modify this distinction, and he got into a certain amount of trouble in orthodox circles.

H.T.: And he had to write a book, *The Splendor of the Church*, to get himself back in.

A.G.: I forget that, but it's possible, because he's still right within the Catholic establishment. But it's a very big question. I think that religion has to be worked out on various levels. On the ordinary level are people who have no time to think about things— which is rather the position, Kobori San told us, of the Soto Zen school. People who don't have time to think about things want, rather, to have a kind of cultus. People who have a bit of time to

think about things want to work religion out scholastically, at
that level. Then there are the people who want to get down to
the fundamentals and experience it all. You get down to the
Catholic mystics and then the Hindu-Buddhist tradition, which
more or less starts where Catholicism leaves off, it seems to me.
But I'd like to switch a little and get you to talk about the medium of poetry as a means of communication. I belong to an old
square school, influenced, before anybody here was born, by Bernard Shaw and others who took the view that it was easier to
write poetry than it was to write good prose. And I'm sure somehow or other that's not true.

G.S.:   Have you read Robert Graves?

A.G.:   Some of him. The impact of his literary personality is so
aggressive that it's a bit distasteful to me.

G.S.:   Are you acquainted with his book *The White Goddess?*

A.G.:   No.

G.S.:   That's an early investigation into the religious roots of poetry. It's rather wrongheaded in some respects. Poetry brings up
the question of primitive and archaic religion, the most archaic
level of religious practice. Graves's thesis is that all poetry belongs to the muse, all poets are servants of the muse, and that
the muse is literally, for him, the Earth Goddess, who was the
great goddess of the neolithic period and the Bronze Age, the
late paleolithic. In a curious way there's a great deal of truth in
that, which I have a hard time articulating. When I say that my
practice is Zen but my position is within Vajrayana, it is because
Vajrayana, of all the sophisticated and learned religious traditions in the world today that I know of, seems to me to be the
only one that has traditional continuous links that go back to the
Stone Age. Actually, Hinduism, Shivaism, has that, too. It's a
tradition that has never made that cut between the pagan and
the present dispensation. Buddhism itself cuts off the earlier dispensation, but Tantrism brings it back in again. These are the
religious insights and practices that belonged to the paleolithic
hunters at the beginning. This is the *real* nature mysticism. People who talk about nature mysticism don't know what they're

talking about. There have been lots more people in the last two thousand years who have been mystics within the terms of "supernatural" mysticism than there have been people who have known what that real nature mysticism is, who have known really what it is to wear the animal masks and to dance the animal steps. And this has been put down—to be realistic, it's what's been called "witchcraft." And Shiva is, if you get back to his historical roots, probably Satan with his horns and his animal worshipers. He belongs to the mythological stratum that the archetype of Satan comes out of. There are all kinds of curious questions that you get into when you start asserting that the powers of the earth and the powers of the underground are valid powers and that your inspiration belongs to them.

I.S.: It can be likened to the statement by Rudolf Otto that the basic sense of religion is awe and wonder, and one cannot feel awe and wonder for something which is known, so it goes to the unknown.

H.T.: Well, the objective of one kind of spiritual life is to get rid of the sense of awe and wonder and to get to an identity. . . .

A.G.: I think at a certain stage awe and wonder come in, but the Enlightenment, the ultimate or most simple response, seems to me: "That's the way it is; that's the truth of things." I want to eliminate—not so much wonder, because that's the beginning of insight, of wisdom—but awe and the sense of fear. Gandhi said so often, "Fear breeds hatred." And Enlightenment seems to bring with it the elimination of fear.

I.S.: Hence the Bodhisattva's gesture of fearlessness, if one has gone through with it.

G.S.: Let's look at it this way, because this sort of resolves it—I can't put it in Christian terms, but I can put it in Hindu terms— the Buddha Dharma strives to escape from the cycle of birth and death, and so does much of the Hindu Dharma. The school of Kali and the Shaktites and some of the Tantric schools accept birth and death in all of its hair-raising possibilities. The poet is right there on that balance, right in there in the area that says "Let the shit fly," which is different from the religious person in civilized times, who is operating in the realm of control, self-discipline, purity, training, self-knowledge.

A.G.: When you write a poem, to what extent, if you analyze it, and I would think you're pretty capable of analyzing it, do you feel yourself the instrument of some muse? To what extent do you feel you have to get down with blood, sweat, and tears, choosing word for word, phrase for phrase . . . ?

G.S.: I haven't had to do that for fifteen years. My discipline as a poet, at least for the last decade, has been a discipline of openness and availableness.

A.G.: It just spouts itself forth, so to speak.

G.S.: Not that easily. The problem is that you have to make the effort when it wants to spout off. It's unpredictable, and it tends to speak at the most inconvenient times, like when you're lecturing to a class or in the middle of a conversation with a friend or riding the bus. That's the discipline that I had to learn. Even to wake yourself up in the middle of the night and put it down. Of course it's learned, because you've applied yourself to all the poetry in the language and trained your ear to it. My friend the late Jack Spicer said, "All poetry is a mixture of static and the real thing." The static is your ego talking, and the real thing is something else talking, and you can hardly tell which is which. But then you have to look at the poem with a ruthless eye. But for everyone I know who works in the realm of poetry, it makes you superstitious, and it makes you something of a gambler, because you can't count on ever writing another poem. You're not relying, in other words, on what you've accumulated in the way of wisdom or skill or reputation—you can only be an instrument of what comes. So all the poets I know are kind of superstitious in the sense that they observe taboos and they feel that there are things they mustn't do; otherwise they're going to cut it off.

A.G.: I'd like to hear articulated the difference between poetry and prose.

G.S.: Prose is the exercise of the rational, humanistic, articulate mind, whereas poetry really is the stuttering voice of revelation.

A.G.: And therefore poetry comes before prose historically.

G.S.: Prose means plain speech—in Latin, *"prosa"*—and, you know, there has always been plain speech.

A.G.: Yes, but not written down, possibly.

G.S.: Neither has poetry required to be written down. Poetry is song. Poetry is what primitive people like the American Indians mean when they say, "I have a death song, and I'll sing it when I'm about to die." Or, "When I went out on my fasting vigil and got my power" (which was when they were about sixteen) "I learned a song. And I won't sing that song except when I'm in great danger or in time of battle." Other times they have a song, which they make up, that is their marriage song or something. But this sense of the song for a specific occasion belongs to the realm of poetry.

A.G.: Then there's the compression of poetry—you can say far more in a short space.

G.S.: But the state of mind that goes with poetry belongs to a very archaic stratum that is part of the mythological mind and has its own discipline and *ascesis*. I have a suspicion that it is what has been called "witchcraft." In Hinduism and Buddhism it's been assimilated. By being called "witchcraft" and finding itself in opposition to the church and the state in the West, it reinforced its negative tendencies. What it was originally was a sophisticated development of paleolithic hunting magic. I have a hunch now that the beginning of Zazen and all yogic practice is hunting. Agricultural magic and agricultural life produce ritual. Look what happens when you switch over from hunting to agriculture. It's a completely different exercise of the intelligence. The hunter has to learn samadhi; he has to practice identification with his quarry. As somebody said, the only way you ever get into the mind of another creature is by wanting to make love to it or wanting to kill it. The two are very close. The hunter learns to know his quarry like a lover. Hunting magic is, as an Indian friend of mine explained, not going out and hunting the animal, but making the animal want to come to you to be killed. A real hunter goes out and he sings his song and he picks his place and then the deer comes, and he shoots it. Anyone who has ever hunted knows that what you have to do is still your mind and sit still. Hunters have to be able to sit still for hours. They have to go out for weeks at a time sometimes. There is a whole practice of mind and body, which belongs to the late paleolithic period.

A.G.:   What about these characters who get themselves done up in pink coats?

G.S.:   I'm not talking about civilized degenerations; I'm talking about the evolution of the race! A hunting culture has a practice of mind and a knowledge that is lost when you enter into agriculture. Just as, it turns out now, the knowledge of the psychedelic herbs, mushrooms, and mistletoe is lost because people quit going into the woods and relying on the forest for edibles, so that apparently a vast amount of knowledge eroded through history. A lot of it survived up through the last century in peasant circles. Things that were known remedies and known psychedelics got lost. . . . But returning specifically to Buddhism:

In my experience the more you practice Zen the more literal the four vows are.

A.G.:   But may I ask who or what is the "I" who vows those particular things.

G.S.:   That's one of those things you have to work on. You see, when you translate it into English you run into this "I." In the Japanese and the Chinese there isn't any "I." It's literally "Beings are numberless; vow to enlighten them. Cravings are countless, or thieves of the mind are countless; vow to cut them down."

A.G.:   How would this do: "Sentient beings are limitless; may they all be saved. Deluding passions are innumerable; may they all be extinguished. The gates of the Dharma are countless; may they all be entered. The Buddha way is supreme; may it be followed."

G.S.:   The verb actually is "vow."

A.G.:   I don't see how in any realistic way an individual can vow to save all sentient beings. He can vow to lend a hand, do his best.

G.S.:   That's what I thought, too. I didn't think I had to take it seriously. This is the way Buddhist practice creeps up on you, though Christian practice has its unrealities too, I'm sure. It creeps up on you to the point where you think, "How am I going to save all sentient beings? What does it really mean to master all the Dharmas?" Then you begin to get the sense of what is meant by dedicating all your future lives to the work of the Dharma.

A.G.: In what realistic sense can you say "all your" or "all my" future lives? As Coomaraswamy says, "The only transmigrator is the Lord," the Buddha.

G.S.: So, we are all the Buddha transmigrating; acting out this complex Dharma drama.

I.S.: Lila. The divine play.

G.S.: That's another angle.

A.G.: Can anything be said in this context about the points of emphasis of the Buddhist ethic as opposed to the Christian ethic? As I understand it, the Christian ethic is conformity given by an external authority, divine law, which, according to the Christian pattern—by fidelity and as a result of mystical experience—can be assimilated into the personality so that it becomes autonomous law, so that the person is leading a pretty well-integrated life. But do any points stand out—is there a greater freedom or a greater strictness in the Buddhist approach to conventional ethical problems?

G.S.: Does Christianity have an absolute ethic really?

A.G.: Personally I'm inclined to think not, except in the term that anything that serves to aggrandize the ego at the expense of other people is wrong. Apart from that I'm not sure that ultimate Christianity would consider anything to be wrong.

G.S.: Is there any basic difference between Christian ethics and, say, Hindu-Buddhist ethics?

A.G.: Not as I have stated it. But I wonder if Hindu or Buddhist thinkers have any criticism from their point of view of the way Christian ethics operate. Do they regard Christian ethics as too ideological, too puritanical, say?

G.S.: I think they would not separate their view of Christian ethics from Christian dogmatics. For instance, the Church has controls and views on individual behavior, like the issue of birth

control, that don't necessarily fall within the scope of basic
Christian ethics stated in the simplest terms.

A.G.:   Probably at the basic level there's no real difference.

G.S.:   There is the difference that the Hindu-Buddhist tradition
says that the killing of all creatures is to be avoided, whereas I
understand the Judaeo-Christian ethic to be concerned with the
killing of human beings.

A.G.:   That's right. They have been involved in a sacrificial system
that is very cruel to animals. What you find in Christianity is a
tremendous sense of guilt and unhappiness and anxiety about
individual so-called misdemeanors and shortcomings.

G.S.:   That is absent in the Far East, and India, too. Ordinary people and even priests and monks don't seem to reproach themselves too severely for individual shortcomings. Scruples are not
as a rule very strong.

A.G.:   It's really a form of egoism or inverted pride. The idea is
"Here am I, a creature who has offended an infinite God." That
kind of thinking doesn't enter in, does it?

I.S.:   I have a feeling it is bound up with something else. We are
much more consciously individuals.

A.G.:   "We" being who?

G.S.:   Western people.

I.S.:   As such we have abstract moral problems of good and evil.
The average normal Far Easterner is more a member of the family or the group and less an individual. The Far Easterner knows
good and evil, but he cannot conceive of it as an abstract moral
problem. That being so, the sense of guilt, of course, cannot
enter.

D.F.:   In Rinzai Zen, so far as I've come to understand it, a feeling
of excessive regret or a feeling of guilt is in fact a hindrance to
one, because the thing to do if you see that you've done something wrong is not to do it again, and that's plenty.

A.G.:   What would be the criterion of whether you've done anything wrong or not?

D.F.:   I think it's the same as it is with us—you feel that something's gone wrong; it's a function of your conscience.

G.S.:   You're dodging something there. What's your conscience?

Does that belong to the realm of the Dharma or to social condi-
tioning?

A.G.: Take an example: in certain circumstances somebody would
think it wrong to make love to another person's wife and somebody else wouldn't think it was wrong.

G.S.: We're in that situation in Western culture today, where
there is no consensus of morality on all sorts of issues. The traditional Buddhist approach has been to get along with the morals
of your society insofar as they don't run too counter to the
Dharma and set up a new practice. But that's assuming a culture
that knows what its own values are. There is nothing in the history of Buddhism to prepare you for the contingency of a society
that doesn't have any clear values of its own, which leaves the
field wide open.

A.G.: And it may be a better situation. . . .

G.S.: It's a genuinely spiritual situation, one that poses an investigation of everything for everybody. It's one of the most beautiful
things about our age that everybody has to make it up for himself, what he's going to do. It's also one of the most painful
things about it.

A.G.: I think that's where Buddhism and existentialism come together—that's what I'd like to try to work out a bit.

G.S.: The Buddhists in Asia haven't been faced with this. They
still say, "Well, they don't listen to their teachers and to their
parents." There are, of course, many people in the West who
consider themselves to be liberal and are by some standards liberal and are by other standards old left. I've talked to old nine-
teen-thirties Communist party members around San Francisco
who are still party members. For instance, my brother-in-law is a
longshoreman, and sometimes I go around with him and talk
with these Communist party people or ex-Communist party people, most of whom have teen-agers or kids in college now. They
say, "These kids, all they do is take dope nowadays. Sheer
anarchy."

H.T.: Diana Trilling wrote an article in *Encounter* saying, "In our
time we were out there. . . ."

G.S.: In our time we were out there doing something!

G

H.T.: Now they're all sitting and watching Dr. Leary found a new religion.

A.G.: Alan's going to found a new religion in San Francisco, I understand.

G.S.: Which Alan?

A.G.: Alan Watts.

G.S.: Is he going to start a new religion?

A.G.: Called Hum. On September fifteenth in San Francisco.

H.T.: He's not founding it; he's just drawing attention to it.

G.S.: That's nice. What I honestly think is happening in the West is not the importation of Hinduism or Buddhism or anything else. I think it's a new religion starting, actually. I have a weird feeling that this is the beginning of a new spiritual epoch.

A.G.: A new religion without a founder, that's very interesting.

G.S.: There have been a lot of religions without founders. It's only these latecomers on the scene, like Islam and Christianity and Buddhism, that have founders. Religion doesn't need a founder.

A.G.: But it needs somebody with a little more insight than the rest of us to stimulate it, perhaps.

I.S.: Or perhaps someone eventually to formulate it.

G.S.: Well, look at how most of Hinduism is mythological formulations by people whose names are unknown. Who wrote the Puranas, or the Brahmanas, or the Upanishads? They were some great minds but they didn't bother to leave their names around in history. One of the most beautiful things in the younger generation today is to be anonymous.

H.T.: They change their names, too.

G.S.: They change their names, they quit using names completely.

A.G.: Who is this?

G.S.: The sub-culture. There is a powerful force toward anonymity in the sub-culture. In the musical circles, amongst the artists and painters and in the groups, they change their names, and nobody will tell you his surname. When they produce works of art they won't put down who did it. And they look on people like myself and my generation, people who write poems and have their names on poems and have books published, they look on that as old-fashioned, and I have a feeling they're right.

H.T.: The lawyers are going to have a terrible time when these people are rich.

G.S.: The bibliographers, too. Have you looked at any editions of the newspaper *The Oracle* in San Francisco? The eclecticism of that is extraordinary. Yet the people who edit it and read it don't have any sense of that. Astrology, Hinduism, Christianity, Saint Francis, Saint John of the Cross, Zen, mantras, American Indians, Vajrayana—everything is fed into that, and it makes a whole in the minds of people who read it. They sell fifty thousand on the streets of San Francisco, and they can't keep up with the demand. One of the differences between this bunch and the people in the fifties is that the beats turned to Zen because they could do that and still call themselves atheists, and the young kids today are unabashedly religious. They love to talk about God or Christ or Vishnu or Shiva. The idea of being religious or spiritual is completely in harmony with them. They don't feel any necessity to pretend that there isn't a soul or there isn't a god or there isn't a possibility of personal devotion. They go very much in the direction of Krishna. The whole Krishna mythology and devotionalism is very attractive to these people, just as it is to these young Japanese. Last Christmas when I was in San Francisco three or four people called me up on the phone, and I thought they were saying "Merry Christmas," but they were saying *"Hari Krishna."* That was their joke on Christmas Day. Pike, for example: the hippies in San Francisco are very turned off by Bishop Pike, because he's so unreligious. They say, "What's wrong with that cat? Doesn't he understand about the Assumption of the Virgin? It's very easy to understand." There're all kinds of levels on which you can understand that theme, and he's very earnestly saying, "This is something in all conscience I'm not sure that I can accept." They say there's no problem in that, you know—like wow! There she goes!

A.G.: Very nice. That's what I found at that hippie party I went to with Gavin. There were a whole lot of hippies with guitars, and I was there in a dog collar. It didn't faze them in the slightest. I felt much more at ease with them than I do at an East Coast cocktail party.

G.S.: Well, they thought you were a hippie in costume. Another aspect is the hippies' outlook on sexuality. They absolutely are not interested in celibacy as part of any practice whatsoever. This is really significant; nobody had thought about it much yet.

A.G.: You have to get around to it sooner or later—to thinking about it, I mean.

G.S.: They'll accept just about anything you suggest—non-violence, vegetarianism, fasting—but they won't accept celibacy.

A.G.: I don't know how that's going to be sorted out.

H.T.: How is it sorted out in Kyoto among younger unmarried people who practice Zazen assiduously?

G.S.: In Japanese culture as a whole, so far, there isn't much sexuality to begin with.

A.G.: They're pretty asexual, are they?

G.S.: So far. I think the scene's changing. But it's common and proper for intelligent girls to go through college and not to have any knowledge of the opposite sex at twenty-four or -five, until they get married, and the same is true for young men. And the young people who live this way do not feel as though they are being put upon particularly. It's really very strange—it's as though they had no particular sexual drive, even during adolescence. And young girls and boys of sixteen to nineteen in this country look and act as though they were five years younger by American standards. So that a Zen monk, for example, enters a monastery at twenty, when he gets out of college, and is there till he's twenty-five. Then he leaves the monastery and gets a temple. Now from twenty to twenty-five a huge per cent of Japanese males have no sex life, so that it can't be said that the boys in the monastery, in terms of the society as a whole, are suffering any extraordinary restrictions. After they leave the monastery and become temple priests in their own right, they generally marry nowadays. So the problem has not really reared its head here yet. The life of Japanese youth is much more sedate than the life of Western youth.

A.G.: They sublimate their sexual drives, do they?

G.S.: I don't know *what* they do with them. I have a lot of Zen monk friends who are very frank, and I've seen a lot. And there really isn't any rule-breaking or sneaking out or having girl friends, prostitutes, or homosexuality of the slightest sort. Have you ever seen any, Dana?

D.F.: No.

G.S.: Of course, living in the monastery you could have two beautiful girls on each side of you and you're too exhausted when the end of the day comes for anything to be done about it.

A.G.: That may be the secret of it: the life is so rigorous that they don't have any energy left. But Father Dumoulin in his history of Zen Buddhism implied the contrary.

G.S.: About the Soto sect. Indeed he did; I noticed that. And it may be true. When they had larger monasteries, and when they had more time, there may have been some homosexuality then.

I.S.: Also, until the Meiji era, temple priests could not be married; now they can be, and that makes a lot of difference.

G.S.: In Tibet there is a great deal of homosexuality, which is accepted because they don't interpret the Buddhist precept about sexuality to include sexual relations with other people of the same sex.

A.G.: I understand that holds good for Hinduism, too, in a good many sects in India. Homosexuality is just part of the scene.

G.S.: It may also have been the case in China and Japan. But again, homosexuality is rather common in Japan, but there are no homosexuals in Japan.

H.T.: As in Greece and Italy.

A.G.: You mean it's not a kind of covert thing.

G.S.: It doesn't become an exclusive variety of sexual behavior. Nor does it become an identity by which you live. It simply is something you do sometimes. There's plenty of evidence of that, even erotic homosexual novels from the Tokugawa period and evidence about that kind of relation between older tea masters and young tea acolytes and in the samurai world as well. At any rate, the situation in Japan today, for all its modernization is, socially and morally speaking, not nearly the same as what is happening in the West. These basic problems of family and social structure haven't really come up.

A.G.: Looking at the people, you get the impression there's much more character, much more solidity to them—serenity, in a way. There's not the boredom and the kind of angst, non-advertence to what they're doing. I noticed at the International House in Tokyo, where we stayed, a little waitress around the table. They're tending to what they're doing.

G.S.:   They really are.

A.G.:   Whereas you can tell in an American restaurant by the expression on waitresses' faces—this is just a job, and their thoughts are miles away.

G.S.:   Well, this is both the strength and the weakness of Japanese culture, I think. Because with that resignation, which is what it amounts to, there also goes a resignation about one's spiritual state of being and the end of any curiosity and energy in investigating any further, an acceptance of your place in society and in the world.

I.S.:   But if they had accepted their status a hundred years ago, they would not be what they are today.

G.S.:   That's a slightly different question, because what we were talking about, I think, was individual states of mind.

I.S.:   I really don't think there is much "individual state of mind." If a mass emotion sweeps, then everybody gets going.

G.S.:   There's a collective energy and a collective ambition and an enormous collective ego in Japan.

I.S.:   Because the collective ego is so strong, the individual in Japan is practically non-existent.

G.S.:   So that if you are going to spiritualize Japan, you have to spiritualize the collective ego.

A.G.:   There has been a terrific transformation here, hasn't there, in the social, political, and economic situation in this generation? Japan is now the third- or fourth-wealthiest nation in the world, I understand—I think after Russia and the United States come West Germany, England, and Japan.

D.F.:   With respect to the gross national product.

A.G.:   Yes, but not with respect to individual incomes.

D.F.:   Per-capita income is down in twenty-third or twenty-fourth place.

G.S.:   Who's got all that money?

H.T: The industrial combines.

A.G.:   The Mitsubishi?

G.S.:   Japan is a classical capitalist nation.

H.T.:   There aren't any antitrust laws?

G.S.:   Hardly: the government is a trust.

A.G.:   And they're making a lot of money out of the Vietnam war, as they did out of the Korean, I understand.

G.S.:   Japanese people as a whole are proud of any success the nation has regardless of what that success means in terms of international morality.

Conversation between Fujimoto Roshi
and Dom Aelred Graham at Eiten-ji Temple,
in the mountains an hour from Osaka,
September 6, 1967.

Sumiko Kudo translated.
Tetsuya Inoue, the temple master, was also present.

A.G.:   I am very pleased to be a guest at Eiten-ji Temple. I was
wondering how long ago this temple was built.

T.I.:   About six hundred years ago.

A.G.:   We have been visiting a number of exponents of the Rinzai
Zen tradition. Now we have the opportunity to learn about Soto.
Could the Roshi tell us about some of the distinguishing fea-
tures of Soto Zen?

F.R.:   I have to talk about the characteristics of Soto Zen in comparison with Rinzai, naturally. First of all, in Zen we have the
koan. There are two kinds of koan: Gen-jo koan, a kind of
natural koan; and Kosoku koan, a verbal formula, made by
man, but not artificial. In any case, Enlightenment is the very
basis of Zen, the foundation. Without Enlightenment it cannot
be Buddhism. In Buddhism we talk about ignorance. Ignorance
is the cause of all sins and sufferings, all evils, we say. In Christianity, I understand, you talk about sin. In Buddhism we don't
talk much about sin, but we talk about ignorance. We say that
because of ignorance there are sins, so we try to get rid of sins by

taking away our ignorance. In order for us *not* to be ignorant, we have to be enlightened. All the Buddhist schools, whatever schools they may be, are based on this Enlightenment experience of Sakyamuni Buddha. In some schools they may talk about doctrine; some of them may be based on particular sutras—Buddha's words; and in some they may practice recitation of Buddha's name. Some talk about Buddhist precepts. They say that the way of Buddhist life is to follow all the detailed precepts. It is Zen that places particular stress on Enlightenment. But whatever school, they are all fundamentally based on the Enlightenment experience.

And I have to say there have been no Buddhists, monks or priests, who came to the Enlightenment experience by way of precepts or doctrine. The Enlightenment experience is the basis. Sakyamuni studied a lot as a prince in the palace, and he tried to follow the precepts, too. But he concluded that all this wouldn't bring him to the Enlightenment experience. He had a very luxurious and easy life as a prince in the palace. He was even ready to go into the ascetic life. For the prince it almost meant death, but he even dared to do that. Yet, by ascetic training he couldn't reach Enlightenment. The ignorant person has all the ego-consciousness, self-consciousness, self-centered consciousness, and all the prejudices. Human beings talk about being the most supreme beings in the world. That's prejudice on the part of human beings, too. When that ego-centeredness or these prejudices are gone, that is the true no-self. And if one comes to the true no-self, then it means that he is back to the original self. We say ignorance is Enlightenment, or Enlightenment is ignorance, or ignorance equals Enlightenment, or ignorance is at once Enlightenment, or something like that. But most people take this statement as a logical or conceptual conclusion. They talk about this and that, all metaphysical discussions, and afterward they say ignorance is at once Enlightenment. These are just conceptual conclusions. But in the case of Buddha, by seeing the morning star he came to have the Enlightenment experience, not as a conceptual conclusion, but by seeing, by sight perception, by the eyes. There are many other masters who came to that Enlightenment experience by hearing some sound, or by smell, or by taste. There are not too many who came to the Enlightenment by taste; but by feeling there are many. All these masters came to Enlightenment. Before that they thought that to see beautiful ladies might be a kind of obstacle in training—perception by the eyes is a kind of hindrance, they thought—but Buddha came to Enlightenment by seeing the morning star. So perception is not an obstacle, but Enlightenment.

Enlightenment by perception: this is one aspect of the Gen-jo koan—the natural koan, which is the koan of daily life too. Every detail of our daily life is a koan in that case. At a very early stage, before the modern so-called koan system was established, the early masters came to have their Enlightenment all by themselves, without any given koan in the form of a problem. So we can say that all the early masters came to their Enlightenment by the Gen-jo koan. But in the course of history some of the masters, through their compassion, observed that this master came to his Enlightenment by such and such a perception, and that master came to his Enlightenment by another perception, and they thought that it might help the people who come to Zazen if they gave examples as a kind of problem to the beginner. That might help or induce him to come to Enlightenment. From this kind of compassionate intention, all the examples of the old masters, how they came to their Enlightenment, were written out. Then the system was worked out that one of the examples in the text would be given to the beginner when he first came to study Zen. These written examples are called Kosoku koans, written-out koans. In the Rinzai school, when the beginners come, they are given one of these koans. In Soto they say every detail of our daily life is the koan itself; so they don't give any particular koan. They don't refer to any examples of the old masters. They are just taught to do Zazen. In Rinzai some example of an old master is given, and the beginner is told not to reach the answer by conceptual or metaphysical thinking or philosophical thinking, but to have the same experience as the master in that koan did. If the koan is by a master who came to Enlightenment by smelling the scent of a blossom, then the disciple has to have the same experience.

In most cases, Mu is given as the first koan, because it helps a great deal to come to the point directly. There are over one thousand seven hundred koans altogether, but some of them are almost metaphysical koans. After all, there can be just one koan, Mu—nothingness should be good enough. Some masters tend to say to the student that he has passed it when he has not passed it. These masters tend to give one koan after another to the disciple. In that way even though the disciple may not have fully understood or fully come to Enlightenment, he may be given a kind of sanction that he has passed the first koan, then the second and third; and after he has passed two hundred koans or so, some masters may give a kind of Inka to him. The master's intention may be to wait for something real to take place in him. Very often it is hard for beginners to concentrate while sitting, so they are advised to put the mind on their palm and concentrate on it.

A.G.: That was Dogen's advice, wasn't it?

F.R.: Yes. In Rinzai, the koan Mu is given; in Soto, the advice is to put the mind on the palm. Both have their weak points. In Rinzai, although the emphasis is always on experience, the tendency is to get very conceptual and metaphysical. All the koans are in some cases treated as conceptual problems. In Soto, they talk about nature, and every detailed item of our daily life is the koan itself. They talk much about daily practice in whatever we do, manners and etiquette, how we live, how we walk, how we do this and do that. Sometimes they even get very strict about how we move around. In Rinzai they work with a Kosoku koan, a written-out koan; what is most important is to have the spiritual, the enlightened, eye, to see through it. Without it one cannot have the real spirit of Zen. In Soto, the *mind* is most important: the faith or mind to live in the way that is the most important. In Rinzai, the strongest term of abuse is "You haven't got the spiritual, the Zen, eye." That is the worst phrase we can use to a monk. In Soto, "You haven't got the Dharma mind" is the worst possible phrase.

A.G.:   That to me is a very illuminating, helpful exposition. If I understand it correctly, the Rinzai koans tend to be verbal and conceptual, whereas you might say that the Soto koans tend to be existential, ordinary everyday life. I would like to go back now and ask a question about the heart of Buddhism. As I understand it, you said that Enlightenment lay in the removal of ignorance, and you contrasted that somewhat with Christianity, with the concept of sin. I would say that Christianity—Catholicism, anyhow—believes that sin is basically ignorance, but ignorance for which the individual is often responsible—often, not always. And Enlightenment consists of knowing one's true self. I would like to ask, What is the true self?

F.R.:   First, some further illustrations of weak points on both sides. In Rinzai, because the emphasis is always on Enlightenment, people may have insights and high spirituality, that is true, but they may not care very much about details. In Soto, there are many monks who as people may be very nice, and their behavior may be perfect, yet they do not have the spirituality to see things through, or they may lack the philosophical basis. These two schools look very different these days, especially from the viewpoint of training. But basically they are one. They are not two different schools; they are both Zen. Dogen, the founder of Japanese Soto, studied or practiced Zazen with the Kosoku koan. It's true that the Kosoku koan is based on the natural koan; so they are not two different things. But nowadays the Soto schools talk about Rinzai as if it were their enemy, and sometimes regard the koan as especially inimical. They talk very much and do their best to make their daily life perfect, but often they do not have insight. That is the weak point. Because for the Gen-jo koan, the natural koan, there is no written text, at the university when they study Buddhism at all, even today, they refer to Sanskrit originals or Pure Land texts. But since all the written-out koans are the result of the natural koan, why not use them and study Zen from them? That is my opinion. Nowadays the Soto school considers everything about Rinzai as being against their school; that's a very weak point of Soto. The weak point in Rinzai is that the original of their koan is the Gen-jo koan, nature and every detail of life, but they somehow forget about this connection. Some particular masters give approval to disciples quite easily, and the disciple may pass from one koan to another. He may come to a so-called Inka quite easily, but his true Enlightenment, true Satori, is very slow in coming, even though he may insist that he has Satori already. That is a very weak point in Rinzai.

Hakuin, who was a great Zen Master in the Rinzai sect, thought he had reached Satori when he was young. He went to have it tested by a Zen Master, who denied it. Then he contracted tuberculosis, and he had a difficult time. To have it cured he went to Kyoto, where he tried all sorts of things. Finally he heard of a hermit living near the Golden Pavilion Temple. This man was not a Zen monk, just a lay hermit. He advised Hakuin to take up Soto Zazen—to put the mind in his palm. By that his illness was somehow cured, and by that he came to his true Enlightenment. This adviser, however, was only a hermit, though a great one, and not a Zen Master. So Hakuin went to Osaka and found a Zen Master who testified to his Enlightenment.

Dogen on his Enlightenment said, "My body and mind have dropped away." Putting the mind in the palm may well be the last stage, regardless of Rinzai or Soto. There may be some few real Zen Masters who have come to this Satori, true Satori, this way—but all these are left as they are, without any worked-out koan, so it does not mean that all of them have this Satori. There are many who do Zazen all right, but do not have this spiritual life.

A.G.: Many Zen Masters?

S.K.: Here the term "Zen Master" may be different.

A.G.: Could there be a Zen Master in Soto who has not had Satori?

S.K.: "Master" is not a fixed title.

A.G.: But it's the same as Roshi, isn't it?

S.K.: Not necessarily. Roshi is a fixed stage. In Soto it's a senior, so he may be an enlightened one or he may not. There is no definition there.

A.G.: I see. A master would know in Soto when a person has been enlightened, is that right?

S.K.: We don't have to talk about it, so we don't ask that question. It's personal. So we don't bother whether one has Satori or not. One may be bothered about one's own question, but not somebody else's.

A.G.: I thought that through discussion it emerged that a Zen Master can tell . . .

S.K.: In Rinzai, yes.

A.G.: But not in Soto?

S.K.: No. The point is just to do Zazen. The role of the master in Soto is quite different; it is to make one do Zazen. So the master doesn't necessarily have to see through to whether one has Enlightenment or not.

F.R.: In Soto "Roshi" is merely the title of a senior so there are many who may not have enlightened eyes.

A.G.: Yet they are called Roshis.

F.R.: In Rinzai, too, although one may call himself a Roshi, he may *not* have the true Enlightenment. That is also quite possible.

A.G.: That is something quite new for me.

S.K.: Oh, but it's apparent to us. Sometimes one claims himself to be a Roshi, but from what he is doing we can see he is not a real Roshi.

A.G.: Well, I'm learning; I didn't realize that.

S.K.: We don't *say* that he is not a true Roshi, but most people know.

A.G.: I would like to express my gratitude and appreciation of what you are saying, which is most illuminating. But I would like to ask another question: What is one's true nature? You said that Soto is concerned with leading the perfect life. What is the perfect life? Is it the perfect moral life, or what?

F.R.: The true self: it cannot be the object of conception or speculation. If we start talking about what is the true self, it is a mistake. Because of ignorance, we start to distinguish between subject and object and talk about the self as if it's a kind of subject which can be perceived, different from others. This self-consciousness is all illusion. The so-called true self is not something we can grasp or define or speculate about. In other words, and the expression may not be good; it's the universe itself. Because of ignorance, we talk as if there is the self here. Ignorance is the cause of all the difficulties and troubles.

A.G.: In regard to that, who or what is it that is seeking Enlightenment?

F.R.: It's the ignorant self who is seeking Enlightenment.

A.G.: The illusory, non-existent self—is that right?

F.R.: Because one is having a dream, one is ignorant. But the master of the dream itself, the real nature, is not ignorant. Once one is awakened to the truth, he is out of the dream and he is not suffering any longer. But as long as he is having the dream, he is living with dualistic contradictions and so is suffering. The enlightened life, that *is* the perfect life. Whatever an enlightened man does, that is the perfect life itself; as with Sakyamuni. It's not easy for anybody to see what is the perfect, enlightened life, so all the details of the Enlightened One's life were written down by the founder of Soto. Those who have not yet reached this Enlightenment are told to follow the written-out details of daily life, to follow what he did. There are many detailed rules and speculations. Each monk and Soto Buddhist is supposed to follow as much as possible each detail. At the very beginning of training in Zen, Soto starts with faith—faith in what Sakyamuni Buddha, the founder, said. Doubt—the "great doubt," we call it—about the problem of man, the human situation and human destiny, is the great problem in the beginning of Rinzai training. Faith and doubt—they sound utterly contradictory. But after all they are one and the same. If one starts doubting, having a rather ordinary sense of doubt, which gets "solved" somehow, in the ordinary sense of the word, and moves from one position to another, then it will take him nowhere. If one really doubts, if one's doubt is the true doubt, he would doubt and doubt and doubt. He would be the doubt itself. There would be nothing else but the doubt. And this would mean that doubt has no objective. The doubt which has no objective cannot be doubt. So it is after all the same as faith.

A.G.: And then the faith has no objective either, is that right?

F.R.: The faith has to be without any objective also, that's true. But again that's a conceptual conclusion. It is impossible for the beginner. It has to come to that point, but at the beginning it means faith in Sakyamuni Buddha and in the founder, Dogen. And also in the present teacher. In Zen we have no so-called sacred writings or sayings on which to rely. Interpretations of sayings or writings may vary from time to time in accordance with history, but what Zen talks about is always fact. The teacher is supposed to be the one who transmits the true teaching of Buddha and the founder. Very often there are teachers who do not. Still, those teachers, even though not living examples, can transmit it. We can listen to Sakyamuni or the founder's teaching through them. The true teacher is the one who has the real experience, who has actually had the *fact* of the experience, so that it came not just through books. In Zen, to study under a teacher and listen to his teaching is very important, not book-reading. If there is any objective, that faith cannot be the real faith—in Buddhism at least. If it has an objective, it is already in the dualistic world. We talk about the self because we are ignorant and in a dream, and we think that there is the objective of training or discipline. But if we are no longer ignorant and we come to the true self in the true sense of the word, there would be no objective. In other words, there would be no objective for training either, except to return to the Dharma.

A.G.: That tallies with my own understanding of it.

F.R.: There is a phrase—*Hachijo no dotoku*. That is, in Zen, as I said, there is no goal. If there is any objective in training or religion, that means there would be a goal. Since there is no objective, there won't be any goal. If doubt in Rinzai is taken in the very shallow sense of the word, and if the koan is understood in that sense, the solution of the koan seems to look like a goal. But that is a great mistake. With faith itself—that is, faith in the true self—there can be no objective and no goal. The same thing can be said of true doubt. Every day, every moment, as time goes on is the time of faith and time of doubt. So there should be no goal in Buddhist life.

A.G.: Would you think it possible for a Christian to be an enlightened person?

F.R.: If one clings to the idea of Christianity and Buddhism, there won't be any true Enlightenment. All these distinctions . . . Religions are in the course of progress now. Christianity and Buddhism seem to be two different religions. And one may talk about Enlightenment from this side or that. But after all, truth, fundamental truth, is just one. If one realizes that point, there is real Enlightenment. But if we talk about *Buddhist* Enlightenment from the side of Christianity, or something like that, this kind of distinction won't lead one to Enlightenment.

A.G.: Therefore, if one distinguishes between Christianity and Buddhism at the conceptual level, then we are not near the ultimate truth of things. To realize the true self is the objective insofar as we have an objective. I would like to ask if you see any relation between the true self and what Christians mean by God.

F.R.: I don't have any clear picture of the Christian God at all. So I can't compare or I can't tell you the relationship between them. But I will speak from the viewpoint of the true self, so you can compare it yourself with your God. I said earlier that the universe itself is the true self. But if I resort to this kind of expression, people start to think of the void—the boundless, limitless universe—and think that equals the true self. That is mistaken. There is no boundlessness, no universality, nothing of that sort of conceptual thinking. This self—I point to myself—is the true self itself. Apart from this self, there is no heaven, no earth, no Divine, nothing. But because this self has the ego-centered self-consciousness of the small self of each individual, this ceases to be just this, me. When we come to realize that this is the true self itself, that is the time we become the Buddha. If we start to describe it, if we start talking about particular features or universality or boundlessness or all these characteristics, everything of the true self is gone. Even when we start talking about space-time relationship, it's all gone. When we start talking about it as the object of studies, and when we describe it as at once the universe or oneness or manyness or something like that, then still it's apart from the true self itself.

As to the relationship of the true self and God, I can say this much: If you describe the true self as similar to God or different from God, the usage of the word "god" is far from the true self altogether in the Buddhist sense of the word. We say the one who has faith in this teaching and who has himself experienced the true self is called a Buddha. Sakyamuni Buddha is one, not the only, Buddha. There is the word "god," such as guardian gods, in Buddhism, too, but there the word has quite a different sense from Buddha. In many cases these gods in the Buddhist tradition have supernatural powers or mystical, superhuman powers. And the fact that they have particular powers or features means that they are still in the dualistic realm.

A.G.: When one says *this* is the true self, what does *this* refer to?

F.R.: *This* is *this!* That's all. It doesn't mean a person or anything else. This is this, that's all. This self at any time can be a Buddha. Or, if one strays from the path, he can be a demon. This doesn't mean that in future time he will be this; there is no time relationship. *This* can become a demon or a Buddha. In Buddhism we, too, have the word "hell," or the world of craving creatures. This doesn't mean there are some other worlds; it means that the state of mind of this self can be hell, or the craving world.

A.G.: Could you say something about worship in the life of a Buddhist?

F.R.: To add a little more in answer to your previous question, the word *"shako"* means suchness, or as-it-isness. These are the expressions given to *this*.

Coming to your last question, various expressions can be given

to worship in Buddhism or in Zen. But plainly speaking, worship
in Zen means the gratitude and respect for Sakyamuni Buddha,
the historical person who achieved the Enlightenment, who became a Buddha, who showed us the way of the enlightened person, and who established the rules for a person to follow who is
not enlightened yet. He is the first enlightened one, or Buddha. I
understand that in Christianity God is the absolute object of
worship. In Buddhism Sakyamuni Buddha is respected and
thanked as the first Buddha, but we can all be Buddhas, and we
can be greater Buddhas than the Sakyamuni Buddha himself.
Sakyamuni was the greatest Buddha so far, that's true, but there
may be a greater Buddha at any moment. So it's a kind of personal, not absolute, worship.

A.G.: Much the same as the Pure Land view, the Amitabha view?

F.R.: We do not worship Buddha as the object of worship. Sakyamuni Buddha is Buddha who experienced Enlightenment. But
in that sense this fan is the Buddha, too, or the true self. So
worship is not of any particular object. Worship is just the pure
act of worship itself. As an item of our training as Buddhists, we
pay our respect and thanks to the historical person Sakyamuni
Buddha, just as we bow to our parents, and say good morning
and good evening and good night.

The teaching of the Pure Land school is a little bit different.
The Pure Land is said to exist in the western direction many
billions of countries away. There was a Bodhisattva called
Hozo, who made forty-eight vows and said that when all were
accomplished the goal of the Pure Land was achieved. Though
in this world, where we are living under adverse circumstances,
we wish to be good, somehow we are not able to. This Pure Land
is the place where there are no adverse conditions at all. Everything is ideal for training. Although one may not be able to carry
on his training in this world, once he is dead he is reborn in the
Pure Land, and there he will have his training where it can be
carried out very successfully. And there, after achieving Enlightenment, he will be a Buddha. Instead of reaching Enlightenment here, Enlightenment will come in the Pure Land. To be

admitted to a university, we have to pass examinations, but in the Pure Land there is a kind of schoolmaster called Amitabha who says there are no entrance examinations in the Pure Land. Just the faith that one will be saved if he recites Buddha's name with the sincerity of his heart—Nembutsu—is needed. He will be born in the Pure Land.

A.G.: And does that give rise to self-power and other power? Those phrases are used sometimes in Buddhist expositions.

F.R.: Amitabha says faith in me saves you. So this can be called the other power. But if there is any intention of trying to improve oneself to be saved, then it's not the other power in the true sense of the word. The other power is not different from no self. In Pure Land it sounds as if Amitabha is the only Buddha, but that is not meant. For the sake of explanation they talk as if the other power is different from self-power, but it's not so. Amitabha is a Buddha, yes, but I myself am a Buddha, and a cat is a Buddha, too. If anyone can perform an act of the true self, he or she is the Buddha, too.

A.G.: I'd like to raise a question on conduct, ethics. Christians try to conform their conduct to some external law given by God or given by the church. That cannot be, of course, in Buddhism. How in practice do Buddhists know what is the right thing or wrong thing to do? What is their rule of action in everyday life so that they know what to do?

F.R.: The concept of ethics does not come into Buddhism. What we talk about is always Enlightenment. If one is enlightened, everything he does is good. If he is not ignorant, he cannot be wrong. In other words, he lives in the domain where there is no distinction between good and evil.

A.G.: Where does the eightfold noble path come in?

F.R.: The word "ethics," or "morals," in the Japanese language is interpreted as "virtues." The eightfold noble path gives the detailed stages of how these virtues may be practiced.

A.G.: I have no more questions. I have reached a state of emptiness.

S.K.: The Roshi objects to your expression. You said you have reached a state of nothingness and you have no questions. Nothingness is not the nothingness in contrast to "yes." So the state of having no questions doesn't mean that you have reached the state of nothingness. Nothingness does not mean just a negation. If it's negation, it's in contrast to affirmation.

A.G.: I was merely playing with words in the Western manner.

F.R.: Where you have no conception of yes and no, being and non-being, that is Mu.

S.K.: I asked the Roshi to speak, and he said, "I have nothing to say. That is Mu."

F.R.: We talk about the ideal, and we usually try to accomplish the ideal. But in Zen there is no fixed, specified, ideal or goal that we have to reach. If there were any fixed goal as our ideal, then there would be a standstill. And if we come to that, it's the end. But the real, absolute truth doesn't have any space or time. It is infinite. The goal is infinite. The present moment is the goal itself. It is the process, it is the stage. In Zen, every moment is *here now*. Apart from that there is nothing. It is the goal, it is the stage, it is the process, it is the absolute. "*Hachijo*" means the eighth stage. For instance, for the sake of explanation let us suppose that there are ten stages. The tenth stage may be perfection, or Buddhahood. In the *Shobo Genzo* by Dogen there is a chapter with the title "*Avalokitesvara*." That Bodhisattva once attained to the tenth stage, to Buddhahood. If he stayed there as the Buddha, he would be perfect; he would have no connection with the dualistic world; he would have no connection with all beings. So after attaining his Buddhahood he came down two stages and he remained in the eighth, the Bodhisattva stage, because of his compassion to save all sentient beings in the world. Although he stays in the eighth stage, that eighth stage is not on his way to the tenth stage, but on his return from the tenth stage. In other words, he is in the twelfth stage! But he is the Bodhisattva of the eighth stage. That is the explanation of *Hachijo*.

S.K.: "*Hachi*" means eight, "*jo*" means stage or accomplishment. In this case it means he was the Bodhisattva who could live the eighth stage.

F.R.: We have another expression: a fluent and able discourse by the man with no tongue. He has no tongue. In the ordinary sense of the word he is not able to speak. But he is *free* to speak. This phrase is often used. "*Hachijo no toku*" and the discourse of the man with no tongue mean one and the same thing. This can be explained as a characteristic of Soto Zen.

I would like to add to what I have been saying. My understanding of the German philosopher Kant may not be correct. But Kant spoke of "the thing in itself." To think of the self-nature as a kind of object of worship like "the thing in itself," is a mistake. Everything is born from "the thing in itself," or true nature; that is true. And this true nature is the origin, or the first cause. But it is not graspable and it cannot be the object of worship. Cats and dogs all come from "the thing in itself," the true nature. But cats and dogs do not have consciousness or awareness of that. To come to the consciousness or awareness of this origin, the true nature, that is Enlightenment. It is like seeds. A seed will develop and change, but the basic quality of the seed will remain as it is whatever form it may take. It will change, but it has continuity, too. And the one who leads his life based on this awakening or this realization is called Buddha. It's just like various lenses. Let us say that we human beings are a blue lens. To realize that we are a blue lens and to live or to work out according to the nature of a blue lens is the life of the enlightened man, the life of a Buddha. The "thing in itself," or true nature, cannot be the object of worship, as I said before. This we call the Dharma Buddha. Sakyamuni Buddha was a historical person who realized this true self and who lived in accordance with this true self. This historical person can be the object of worship.

There may be various kinds of realization, such as psychological realization, scientific realization, and so on. But Zen realization is not the same as these realizations. All other so-called realizations are for us to use to meet all sorts of outside requirements in human life.

As to ethics, we are not concerned with ethics, good and evil, in Buddhism. The true self is neither good nor evil. The function of religion is to let us work out or live in accordance with the true nature, with the self-nature. To be ignorant of the self-nature, or "thing in itself," an outsider may call evil. Suppose I am a fire. If I am fire, to realize the nature of fire is Enlightenment, to come to this awakening and to have the realization of the true nature of fire. To live in accordance with the true nature of fire, that is the life of a Buddha, Enlightenment. To do anything against the nature of fire may be considered evil. For instance, if fire goes into water, it is against its nature. To live according to his true nature is the life of the enlightened man, the life of a Buddha. Whatever he does in accordance with his true nature is good.

The additional comments that follow were later added by Fujimoto Roshi. Because he is almost blind and deaf, he did not feel that the conversation recorded here fully expressed his ideas.

When Dom Aelred Graham visited me on September 6, 1967, I told him before answering his questions: "Intuitively my mentality works quite well, but when it comes to arranging and explaining my thoughts, I am very clumsy. I frequently deviate from the question, and it is not seldom that my verbal expressions turn out to be quite contrary to what I really mean. I am afraid, therefore, that what I am going to answer now may not clearly convey my real intentions." I told him, therefore, that I would, perhaps, write out my comments later. Sure enough, there seem to be many ambiguous points and misunderstandings in my dialogue due to lack of clarification and insufficient explanation. The following are supplementary explanations to what I told him on the occasion of his visit to Eiten-ji.

If I remember correctly, the first question asked by Father Graham was something to this effect: "What do you think of Christianity from the standpoint of Zen?" I rather hesitate to give my frank opinion in this regard, but I will dare to say this: The task of any religion is to transmit divine revelation to man. For this to be done, it is first necessary for the spiritual teacher himself to see God. Even if he cannot do this, he should try to continue his discipline with this aim in mind, with his faith in God always. Christianity today, however, seems to set up a god based on conceptual thinking. This is my frank opinion.

In Buddhism all the conceptual explanations and teachings in the sutras and sastras are likened to fingers that point to the moon. Since the finger cannot be the moon itself, however precisely we may analyze or synthesize it, we cannot define the true moon. We have to leap from the finger to the moon, far in the sky, and directly see the real moon. It is vitally important, therefore, that the pointer himself should have seen the moon. If correctly used, the conceptual explanations are quite effective. If misused, the moon—Buddha—will be lost. Buddhist scriptures refer to this metaphor, but it should be an important guide in studying Christianity, too.

In Buddhism there are, at present, different sects and schools, and their studies have been variously developed. The differences are of a methodological nature, but the aim of all of them is Enlightenment. Buddhism is therefore described as "teaching to clarify one's illusions and awaken one to Enlightenment."

The present situation, where various religions are existent, is a transitional stage toward the one absolute religion. In the distant future, we may have one true religion in which all the different teachings are unified. I think the Absolute should be one and the same whether it be God or Buddha.

Father Graham asked whether it is possible for a Christian to attain Enlightenment. I would say that it is. However, as long as Christians are attached to *the* Christianity, as they have been, it is not possible. The same can be said of Buddhists. That is, the Absolute should have no particular coloring. Correct Zazen, which is the basic practice in the Zen school for bringing about Enlightenment, makes us cast away all attachments and illusions. Therefore, I believe Zazen is the best means to attain true Enlightenment. It can be the basis of seeing God, in whatever religion it might be practiced.

Apropos of our discussion of the meanings of the natural koan,

Gen-jo koan, and the text koan, Kosoku koan, and the differences in studying them, I forgot to mention one important point. Even when a Zen student is studying a text koan, the natural koan should be the direct cause of his actual Enlightenment, his seeing into the truth. Otherwise his realization remains merely conceptual or speculative, which definitely is not right. So although recently most students attain Enlightenment by means of the koan Mu, one really comes to Enlightenment when one of the five sense organs reacts to an outside phenomenon and works as a medium to bring about natural awakening. So, in fact, the disciple attains his Enlightenment by the natural koan.

I should like to refer to the typical Buddhist expressions "Ignorance is at once Enlightenment"—ignorance and Enlightenment are one; and "Life and death are at once nirvana"—the present situation is ideal. The words "are at once" seem to connect two utterly contradicting terms. The truth of such expressions can be proved by the fact that a sense organ works as a medium for Enlightenment.

In Theravada Buddhism, where training based on actual human situations is carried on, the five senses are called "five desires" and are regarded as typical examples of ignorance. In Mahayana Buddhism, which is based on the fundamental principle, the real entities of the five desires are called entities of Enlightenment. This is a very important point. This affirmation is not made as a theoretical conclusion based on conceptual reasoning, but is the report of actual fact, since a sense organ is always the gateway to one's Enlightenment. Enlightenment is made possible when "pure intuition" works. The ordinary term "intuition" is far from "intuition" in Buddhism, because our everyday intellectual life is not pure.

The real goal of Zazen practice, therefore, is in the natural koan, and Shikan taza, pure Zazen without any aim, should be the authentic practice. The koan Mu can be a good means by which to lead students to Enlightenment, since this is a very simple and direct koan. In studying it, however, if any thought on Mu or conceptualization about Mu is involved, this is a mistake. The spiritual effort to avoid conceptualization itself is already a relativistic effort, and it is not possible to attain Enlightenment, which is absolute, by such dualistic means. When Zazen with koan studies has finally become identical with Zazen of the natural koan, real Enlightenment is for the first time attained. It is true that dynamic strength may be lacking in the training if no pedagogical means are used. There are some masters who use text koans. In Soto we use three hundred koans selected by Dogen himself; it is in order and correct to do so.

There is a difference between Soto and Rinzai that I failed to mention in our conversation. In Soto training faith is emphasized, while in Rinzai spiritual quest is important. These two constitute, after all, the two sides of a coin, and the difference is not a fundamental one. In the ninth chapter of a book called *Admonitions for Students*, which was written by the Soto founder, it is said that one should do Zazen with the faith in Enlightenment attained by Sakyamuni Buddha under the bodhi tree when the morning star twinkled. The truth to which Sakyamuni testified does not exist outside ourselves; it is primarily within us. As descendents of Sakyamuni, we should have a firm faith in the teaching of the primary Buddha nature and should do Zazen. It is of course necessary that by Enlightenment one should cast away all dualistic views of Enlightenment-and-ignorance and attain Buddhahood. This is the process that would consequently follow the basic training. Novices should therefore have firm faith in the Buddha's Zazen, which brought Enlightenment to him, and should practice it accordingly.

In Rinzai it is said that three basic elements are required in doing Zazen. First one should have firm faith in the teaching of the primary Buddha nature, as in Soto. Next one should have the Great Spiritual Quest. One has to have a spiritual quest once, in order to have firm correct faith. Third, one should have a strong will and aspiration with which to plunge into the abyss of quest and work with it until he attains absolute truth. It is therefore said that under the Great Quest is the Great Enlightenment. In Rinzai, however, one has to go on searching and seek out the seeking self. Finally there will be no seeking subject existent any longer, but just absolute truth itself. The absolute faith of the Soto school and the absolute quest of the Rinzai school attain the same end, but the Rinzai process is more philosophical and scientific.

During our conversation I referred to "the teaching of the eighth stage" in explaining Buddha. What this phrase means is the avoidance of the tenth stage—static fullness—on the way to Enlightenment. The figure eight is not to be interpreted here as two less than ten. It is, in fact, the twelfth stage, two stages beyond the tenth, or, rather, it is the infinite stage, according to our teaching. It indicates that an end, climax, or goal has not been reached, because if something reaches its termination, it has no room for further development. It will stop working; it will cease to be active and will be dead.

The true absolute is not the conceptualization of the absolute; it cannot be located. It has no relativistic object to which to restrict itself. It has dynamic implications; it is free. The true absolute implies infinite progress. The figure ten is confronted with one, but eight has nothing to confront. Though eight is less than ten, it is absolute because it is not relativistically discriminated. It can go beyond ten and be twelve. Dogen admonished his disciples on actual discipline by referring to this eight. He said, "In mid-way, it is already attained; on completion never are we to stop." The true absolute should be taken in this sense. It is the fulfillment at every moment, every place; it is the completion of non-completion. This is the ideal of Buddhism.

Another question asked in our discussion was "What is Buddha?" In reply to this question I struck my body, shook it, and said, "This is Buddha." Father Graham looked rather surprised and asked for clarification. I lowered my voice and said, "It is just this!" by which I meant that if one fails to find Buddha as it is described by "this" and tries to find Buddha in conceptual interpretation, he is getting far away from the True Buddha. I concluded that in Buddhism everything starts with "this" and ends with "this." Therefore what is actually needed is to be awakened to "this."

There are theological explanations for this. Buddhism teaches that all beings are primarily Buddhas. Everything is a Buddha as it is. Human beings are born as Buddhas primarily—this is the basic principle of Buddhist teaching. Originally human beings are products of Great Nature. There is not a single man who came into this world because of his own will. Where there is no intentional consciousness, there is no dichotomy of subject-object, and in this nonduality, as-it-is-ness of nature is revealed. Then man begins to develop his intellectual life, which is a unique human characteristic. Dualistic discrimination of subject-object is a result of this intellectual function, and human existence can be protected by it. However, such dualism can also be a cause of evil. Generally, life in this phenomenological world depends on helping one another. When intellect excells too much, one begins to favor his own ego. Thus, he makes undue requirements for himself and hurts others, giving rise to real evil. Conflict between subject and object gradually develops into the struggle between nations and races, and finally might involve the whole of mankind, threatening the life of everyone on earth. This is a distorted outcome of dualistic discrimination. In this civilized world everyone should be aware of it, and yet they still accelerate the crises. This is a definite proof that conceptual understanding alone will never solve the problem. There is no other way but to be awakened to "this"—the actual reality that is here represented by "this body"—and then to try to develop it. Since we are lost in ignorance by ourselves, we are to be enlightened by ourselves, too. Any outside efforts and offers are of no avail. It is, after all, just "this" and nothing else.

Religion, generally speaking, is based on God. Therefore one should never lose sight of God as the basis of teaching. I imagine that the meaning of divine revelation in Christianity might be the same as that of the koan. Perhaps in the West they do not resort to such an unusual way of demonstration.

Japan recently had a great philosopher called Kitaro Nishida and a Zen authority named Daisetz T. Suzuki. They often used the expression "realization of nothingness" and "absolute nothingness." There are some Rinzai people who refer to these expressions because they think they may be helpful in theoretically explaining the koan Mu. Since these are terms used by great philosophers, they can be useful as a supplementary means in Zen teaching, provided they are correctly understood and used. They are difficult terms, however, and it is said that even the so-called successors of the Nishida philosophy are unable to fully understand them. So Zen people with no philosophical background should not carelessly use these words. That is why I felt somewhat uncertain of Father Graham's intent when he put an end to his questions with these words.

While Sakyamuni Buddha was alive, he was the only Buddha. With his death, his disciples lost the object of their faith and sought after that "essential something" that had made Sakyamuni the Buddha, in order that they follow the right direction in their training. They also wanted the stability of organization. These requirements gradually resulted in the establishment of the idea of Buddhahood. At first, Buddhahood was based on Sakyamuni himself. That various other Buddhas were sought after as the objects of faith was a later development.

Sakyamuni, who achieved Enlightenment by means of Zazen, declared that his teaching was not his own invention or discovery, but that it had been transmitted by the Seven Past Buddhas from the infinite past. Thus, Sakyamuni did not claim that his teachings expressed his own view of the universe, but a view that he accepted as the historical truth to which he was awakened. He appointed Maha-kasyapa the successor of his organization, after confirming that he had attained the same Enlightenment that he himself had. Dharma transmission in later ages followed the same pattern. In Zen in particular, the transmission of historical truth, spirit, is emphasized. Enlightenment is not the discovery of the objective principle, therefore, but is the realization of the truth of mankind transmitted from the Seven Past Buddhas.

Recently, talk of "historical truth" has not referred to the human truth that existed prior to the existence of its transmitters, the ancestors of man. I think that when we have the Buddhist historical truth, which originates in the Seven Past Buddhas, the life and spirit of man can be united with the great universe and nature.

The term "truth," or "spirit," that I use here does not mean spirit as against material. It is the essence or spirituality that is the source of all the sentient and non-sentient beings in the universe. Beings in this phenomenal world do not realize it. Buddhists accept this great life essence of nature as the primary source of human life, and give it the name the "Seven Past Buddhas," considering it the beginning of human history. Thus, human beings are products of nature and our life is to be in accordance with the truth, the spirit of great nature. In Buddhism this is revered as the Dharma-kaya Buddha.

Everything in the universe, however, has different living characteristics—differences of time, place, and situation. If we disregard such differences and deal with them without due discretion, then the outcome will be the destruction of the universe. In human society, differences between male and female, between races, between regions are to be given due consideration. Furthermore, each individual is differently endowed. These endowments or abilities cannot all be promoted in the same manner, but only in accordance with different time and place. Only when these conditions are well developed, without confusion or mutual destruction, will the whole universe make progress.

In our discussion I used the metaphor of colored lenses and stressed that the light shines through each lens according to the color of the lens. Those who have done their best in accordance with this principle are called "living Buddhas." This classification of Dharma-kaya Buddha and living Buddha was made even in the days of primitive Buddhism.

Sakyamuni was awakened to his true nature when he attained Enlightenment under the bodhi tree. Sakyamuni as he is worshiped in Soto is not the individual by that name, but the symbol of the historical truth to which he was awakened when he achieved Enlightenment. On the occasion of the achievement he declared: "The joy of this great realization is not mine alone. All beings are born with this true nature." Buddhism, especially the Zen school, maintains that such privilege is not limited to beings who lived three thousand years ago, but is true of every one of us today.

Father Graham also asked me if Buddhism teaches ethics, and I answered, "It does not." In Japan the word "ethics" has common-sense connotations. The general understanding of the term is: "Any conventional actions that are considered convenient to the actual living of people are good, and those contrary to them are evil." The standard of ethics is vague and changes easily according to the times, living customs, political changes, et cetera. In Japan, especially before and after World War II, ethical standards were changed and revised several times. The so-called code of ethics did not serve its purpose. Also, the contradictory situation of a world where good people must suffer and bad people prosper gives us the impression that ethics might as well be non-existent. Buddhism does not talk of such relativistic, worthless ethics. Buddhism teaches something more than ethics. This is the reason I said that Buddhism does not talk about ethics.

Father Graham then asked if the Eightfold Noble Path is not an ethical teaching. This is a method by which one can reach ethical ideals, but is not itself ethics. There are some who say that the Eightfold Noble Path enumerates eight items one after another, at random. I personally think that there is a practical order. First it is necessary to have "right seeing," the first item; and then "right thinking," "right ideas," and "right living" become possible.

I came to realize during my conversation with Father Graham that my interpretation of the term "ethics" might be different from his. If so, I have to apologize for my careless conclusion. He might have meant something like Kant's "ethical principle." While I do not know fully what this principle is, I suspect that it may be similar to "ethical ideals" and not the so-called ethics that are used in Japan. In that sense, Buddhism does teach ethics, since, in spirit, Buddhist precepts should be interpreted in the same manner as "ethical ideals."

A Buddhist scripture says, "Action in accordance with Right Dharma is good, and that against Right Dharma is evil." Right Dharma means the truth of real Buddhist Enlightenment. In Buddhism we say that once true Enlightenment is attained, right deeds naturally follow. The Eightfold Noble Path presents actual practical items leading to true Enlightenment. The last item of the eight is "right Dhyana." "Ethical ideals" must belong to the religious sphere, and all the right doings should be carried out in this religious domain. Thus we can truly say that religion is the revelation of God.

My reply that Buddhism does not teach ethics really meant that ethics should not be treated independently from religion.

Visit of Dom Aelred Graham to Abbot Hashimoto of Yakushi-ji Temple in Nara, September 17, 1967.

Professor Masao Abe translated.

The Abbot belongs to the Hosso sect of Yui-Shiki, the Yogacara school of Buddhism.

A.H.: In the West only Zen among many forms of Buddhism is well known. Furthermore, the Zen known in the West is only the Suzuki Zen, rather than the orthodox form of Zen. As far as the orthodox form of Zen is concerned, Suzuki Zen is not sufficient. (Incidentally, Yamada Mumon Roshi may be said to be one of the best Zen Masters in the Rinzai school.) And after all, Zen is only one of the branches, offshoots, of Buddhism as a whole. If you want to know what Buddhism is, you should study the orthodox schools of Buddhism, represented by Nagarjuna, Vasubandhu, and so forth.

A.G.: I am beginning to realize that that is so—that Zen is a particular form of Buddhism that has attracted attention in the West because of the peculiar situation of Westerners being disappointed in their own religious traditions and perhaps finding in the Zen aspect of Buddhism something that answers their spiritual needs and insights without demanding any creed, without having any dogmatic formulations. But I understand that the form of Buddhism that you represent is much older than Zen and lies behind Zen, so I would like to ask for some further insight into it.

A.H.:   What we are doing is studying the most basic principles of Buddhism. So our's is not the study of a particular sutra, or the Vinaya, but the study of the Abhidharma. There are two main currents in Mahayana Buddhism. These are the Madhyamika, represented by Nagarjuna and so forth, and the Yogacara, represented by Ashvaghosa, or Asanga. However, these two schools are based originally on the Abhidharma. So the study of Abhidharma doctrine is most essential.

A.G.:   And the actual meaning of Abhidharma is?

A.H.:   The literal meaning is the "treasure or warehouse of the doctrine." It is the doctrinal study of the basic sutras or scriptures.

A.G.:   The word *"abhi"* adds something to the Dharma or explains the Dharma. What does the actual word *"abhi"* mean?

A.H.:   *"Abhi"* means "to stand against." It may be better to say it in German: *Gegenstaendlich.* "Dharma" means truth, and phenomenal things as well. In this case it means the latter, phenomena or phenomenal world. So "Abhidharma" means taking the phenomenal world as the object of studies.

A.G.:   And the practice of the Yogacara is meditation, is that correct?

A.H.:   The practice of Buddhism as a whole is meditation in terms of samadhi. So meditation is the basic practice for Buddhism in general.

A.G.:   What view does the Yogacara tradition of Buddhism take of Enlightenment? Does that happen suddenly, or is it a long process? Do you know when it's happened? Is there any particular discipline, like a koan, to bring it about?

A.H.:   There is sudden Enlightenment as well as gradual Enlightenment. Sudden Enlightenment may happen for those who are brilliant or very sharp; while gradual Enlightenment may take place for those who are not so brilliant or talented.

A.G.:   It would be a question, then, of intellectual brilliance or talent, would it?

A.H.: In Buddhism three things are always emphasized. These are sutra or sila—law; sutta or Abhidharma—doctrinal analysis, and the principles for daily life—meditation and *prajna,* wisdom. These three are essential. These three must become one at the basis of Buddhist life. So those who are brilliant and sharp are not necessarily those who are intellectually so but those who are good in terms of the oneness of observation, meditation, and learning.

A.G.: Buddhism has a philosophy; you might say an ontology in Western terminology. I've sometimes seen it expressed in the phrase "all in one and one in all." Is that a Yogacara formulation of the matter?

A.H.: Buddhism is *not* philosophy or religion in the Western sense. Buddhism will always start from the standpoint of reality, so it is not a philosophy. Practice is the primary matter. Starting from a practical matter, Buddhism develops itself.

A.G.: Wasn't Nagarjuna a philosopher even in the Western sense?

A.H.: Nagarjuna *cannot* be regarded as a philosopher. He was not a philosopher, but a thoroughly religious man.

A.G.: He had a brilliant, very dialectical mind, did he not?

A.H.: It has been said that there are similarities between Yogacara and the philosophy of Kant and between the Kegon school and existentialism. But it is only a superficial observation. The late Professor Anezaki, of Tokyo University, under whom I studied in my younger days, made a comparative study of Buddhism and Christianity, emphasizing the similarity between them. But from my viewpoint Professor Anezaki just gathered similarities, neglecting the basic standpoint, the basic difference.

A.G.: I understand that there is no adequate statement, in words, of Buddhist doctrine, just as there's no adequate statement of the Christian position. So to that extent they're similar. But still, both try to use words to express themselves. Here in Kyoto I've heard several Roshis say that a grain of sand is the universe. Or this [I held up a cake] is the universe. Would you agree with that?

A.H.: That one is the whole and the whole is one is the teaching of the Tendai and Kegon schools. This may be said, but from my viewpoint it is merely a theoretical view apart from reality. In reality one is not the whole and the whole is not one. So far as we stand on reality we cannot say that one is the whole and the whole is one. The Yogacara and, particularly, the Abhidharma schools are most concerned with this point, namely that one is *not* the whole, the whole is *not* one.

A.G.: You say they *are* concerned with it, or they are not?

M.A.: They *are* concerned with realistic distinctions between things.

A.H.: Abhidharma developed from the fifth century B.C. to around the fifth century A.D., so it has a long history of developing its doctrinal understanding. The theory "The whole is one" may be said to be the culmination of its development. It is not good to say so in an easy way. Before saying so we should study the long history of the development of the Abhidharma school.

A.G.: And what would your comment be on the saying "A grain of sand is the universe"?

A.H.: It can be said from the standpoint of the Tendai and Kegon schools. But in reality a grain of sand is a grain of sand, while the universe is just the universe. So it can be said only theoretically, not practically or actually.

A.G.: That corresponds more with my experience and observation.

A.H.: Such a statement may be uttered theoretically but not practically; and theory and practice always must be one. My own standpoint is based on the oneness of theory and practice, which I think is most important.

A.G.: Is there anything that you think it important for a Westerner, a Christian like myself, to *know* about Buddhism—anything you would like to say, anything you might think most important for a person like myself?

A.H.: Professor Dunn, of London University, who stayed and studied Buddhism with me, may help you in that connection, because I taught him what is most essential to Buddhism. Mrs. Rhys-Davids, who translated the Pali texts into English, might help you.

A.G.: No. I thought perhaps that you would have something *your-self* to say.

A.H.: My spirit is in Maitreya's teaching, which is described in the Yogacara Sutra and also in the book of Asanga. I will never be apart from that teaching. I never compromise myself so far as my own religious standpoint is concerned. The doctrine of Yogacara is my own viewpoint as well as the basis of my daily life.

Discussion at Doshisha University, Kyoto,
under the auspices of Professor Masatoshi Doi,
Director of the National Christian Council Center
for the Study of Japanese Religions,
September 20, 1967.

The Reverend Shojun Bando of Otani University translated when
necessary. Other Buddhist and Christian scholars present were:
Professor Hiroshi Sakamoto of Otani University; the Reverend
Sojyo Hirano, Buddhist priest, Hanazono University; Professor
Raymond J. Hammer of Queen's College, Birmingham, England;
Father Ichiro Okumura of Carmel House of Meditation; Professor
Michio Sato of Ryukoku University; the Reverend Jan van Bragt
of the Immaculate Heart Missions; the Reverend Tokio Kochi of
the Anglican Church; Professor G. G. Lloyd of Doshisha Univer-
sity; Professor Masao Abe of Nara College of Humanities.

DOI: We are very privileged to have such prominent Buddhist
  scholars participating in this discussion between Christianity and
  Buddhism. So, Dom Aelred, would you please give a brief presentation of the central theme of your book *Zen Catholicism?*
A.G.: Thank you very much, Dr. Doi. I am going to be brief and
  speak slowly. I will begin by saying how very grateful I am to be
  here and how appreciative to have the opportunity of meeting
  such a distinguished group of professors and scholars. The original title of the book I wrote was *Zen Catholicism* with a question

mark, raising the question whether there was any possibility of linking Zen and Catholic Christianity. But the publisher persuaded me to let it stand with the title *Zen Catholicism* and the subtitle *A Suggestion*. At the beginning of the introduction to the book I pointed out that Christianity was originally a way of life, implying that it wasn't just a doctrine or a dogmatic system or a system of ethics. Since the early centuries Christianity has become overlaid with a legal superstructure and doctrinal and credal formularies, all of which may have been necessary. But it seems to me that at this time the Western world is in great need of getting to the heart of its own tradition, and the query I raise is whether the Buddhist insight could not help the West in that particular enterprise. It seems to me that the time has come for a radical self-examination by Christians of their own position. I think there is a tradition of violence and intolerance in the Christian scheme of things, which needs to be re-examined and perhaps enlightened by something akin to the Buddhist point of view. I think that the time has come perhaps for everybody, Christians and Buddhists, to ask themselves what the true nature of religion is. It seems to me that there is a dichotomy between religion considered as a system or a way of life preparing one for future bliss in some other world and as a system adapting one to live happily and constructively and compassionately in this world without much regard to the future. Cannot the great religious thinkers be divided roughly into prophets and seers? By "prophet" I mean one who speaks for God and maybe commends or insists on what the will of God is, like the great Hebrew prophets and Jesus of Nazareth himself, who was, of course, also something of a seer. By "seer" I mean a man of insight. The seer Sakyamuni Buddha was also, I suppose, something of a prophet, but was concerned with facing the reality of things in all their aspects. The modern world has to some extent grown a little weary of prophets and needs the light that comes from the seers. So to conclude this brief, very oversimplified summary, the question I raise in my book is not the desirability of those brought up in the Western Christian tradition embracing Buddhism, but whether the Buddhist insight, and the particular concern of the Enlightened One for truth—for reality as distinct from appearances, as distinct from verbal statements—has not something to contribute in greatly helping Christians to realize their own inheritance, their own tradition.

DOI: Questions may be raised from both sides. I myself am now planning to write an article on a comparative study of revelation and Enlightenment. My hypothesis is that revelation and Enlightenment *may* be the two sides of one reality. I am looking in that direction.

A.G.: That should be very interesting indeed.

VAN BRAGT: Father Graham, may I ask you how you came to study Buddhism?

A.G.: I've often been asked that question, and it's just, I suppose, a natural affinity or part of my karma, or whatever way you like to put it. I notice the theological notes I made thirty years ago had parallel quotations from certain canonical Buddhist scriptures, sutras, and so on. And the life of Sakyamuni has always struck me as being in its own way just as fascinating as the New Testament story.

HAMMER: In part of your introduction you referred to the clash or the difference between the seeming violence of Western religious tradition and the non-violence of the Eastern tradition. You related this largely to Buddhism. To what extent would you take this as being already in the Hindu tradition, where you have *ahimsa?* Then, a sort of parallel point: the history of Buddhism in Asia, and in Japan too, is not necessarily a history of non-violence. We are very near Hieizan, and the monks came down from Hieizan and burned up Kyoto many times, and there are rival groups. I just felt at this point that you were drawing things a little too black and white, without taking due regard of the very gray character of all our religious professions.

A.G.: I think that's a very fair comment. With regard to the first point, the relation of Hinduism to Buddhism, I'm reminded of a remark by Ananda Coomaraswamy on that topic. He said that the more superficially you look at Hinduism and Buddhism, the more striking the contrast seems; the more deeply you look into them, the more similar they seem to be. I'm not really qualified to say how accurate that is. About the Christian tradition of violence: it seems to me there's a real *sanction* for it in the Old Testament and part of the New Testament. So that it is a truly Christian activity, as far as the documents go, to conduct a crusade against the Turks, one of which crusades was preached by a Christian mystic, as is the mysticism of Saint Francis of Assisi. I would think there's as much documentary support for either line. I wonder if there is as much documentary support in the Buddhist tradition? Monks, of course, are curious personalities in all denominations. For example, the monks associated with Cyril of Alexandria were no more desirable characters, I think, than the monks who might descend on these parts and set fire to buildings. Neither group, perhaps, appealed very much for sanction to their religion. But it does seem to me that when you get a cardinal of the Roman Church talking, a year ago, about the war in Vietnam being for Christian civilization that the ideological trend in Christianity could be more tempered by a little of the insight coming from the East.

HAMMER: On the other hand, one asks whether he was saying that as a Christian or saying that as an American.

A.G.: I'd very much like to hear the Buddhist commentary on the Zen scene here in Kyoto. I've heard a good deal from Zen Roshis, and I'm sure there's something else from other angles to be said within the Buddhist tradition.

ABE: As I said the other day, in the West, Zen is regarded almost as the only form of Buddhism in Japan. However, it is not true, as I hope you have already noticed. It is true that Zen is one of the important religious ways of life of Japanese in general. But besides Zen, Esoteric Buddhism, Shingon Buddhism, established by Kobo Daishi, Pure Land Buddhism, established by Honen and Shinran, are very popular, particularly among ordinary people. Esoteric Buddhism, Pure Land Buddhism, and Zen Buddhism may be said to be sources or roots of Japanese culture, more or less the basis today. I hope you recognize the variety and diversity that can be found in the religious life and viewpoint.

A.G.: I understand that the Zen Buddhism that is presented to the West even by one or two wandering Roshis is not the Zen Buddhism that is approved of in Japan. I'd be very grateful to hear more of that. I don't know whether it's right to mention names, but I've been told that the Zen that is presented to the West—such as in a book that has come out recently, *The Three Pillars of Zen*, which gives a number of Enlightenment experiences—would not be recognized by the Zen Roshis in Japan. I wonder if anyone feels disposed to throw any light on that.

HAMMER: May I speak for one moment? I think probably the Zen experts should come in. But I would like to say, from my own experience, first, following from what Professor Abe was saying, the very fact that Zen has had as good an English introducer as Suzuki Daisetz has meant that this has been the only part of Japanese Buddhism that has been popularized throughout the world. I think with regard to your second question that the main clash comes in the very understanding of Satori itself. Why Zen attracts many in the West in the first place is because of its apparent logic-shattering effect, that it doesn't follow any patterns of Western logic. On the other hand, many books that present Zen in the West or try to explain the Satori experience insist on using Western philosophical categories, and the use of these categories really negates what Zen is trying to do or be. The fact that they're trying to say that you're neither affirming nor denying, but trying to get beyond the point of ordinary logic, logical affirmations or logical denials, means that you cannot really give a systematic account. And many of the Western accounts are trying to systematize what I think the Zen Roshis here in Japan would want to say cannot be systematized in that kind of way.

A.G.: I agree that that situation exists or has existed in the West. But it's a more precise point within the Zen tradition itself that I'd be grateful to have some instruction about. Namely, I understand that there's a controversy about the way in which the Satori, or Kensho, experience is to be brought about. The book I mentioned, *The Three Pillars of Zen,* which is now available in Kyoto, promotes as the authentic Zen tradition a rather highly charged, emotional, forceful way of bringing about or striving to bring about the Satori experience in the Zendo in the process of Sesshin. And there are a number of Satori experiences or alleged Satori experiences related in that book. Now I have heard it said that that is not regarded by the traditional Roshis here in Japan as the genuine article. That's what I'd be grateful if anybody could comment on. This book is circularized largely in the United States, and its procedures are being practiced there. What I would like to know is how authentic those procedures are with regard to the Zen tradition here in Japan. I understand that there's quite a large controversy in the Buddhist tradition about them. I'm interested in this point of view because I think Father Lassalle, a Jesuit in Hiroshima who has been trying to adapt certain Zen meditational practices to the Catholic framework, had his training, so far as he had training, in that Yasutani Roshi–Philip Kapleau tradition, you see, and that's why it interests me.

ABE: Father Lassalle has practiced Zazen under the guidance of Harada Roshi, who is the teacher, the Master of Yasutani Roshi. So in that sense Father Lassalle practiced Zazen under the master of the master in question. However, Master Harada is appreciated very highly by both Soto and Rinzai schools. I heard that Yasutani Roshi, the master of Philip Kapleau, more or less emphasized the psychological aspect of Kensho or meditation experience. That is the reason why many Americans rather easily approach his guidance, and at the same time it is a question of the genuine point.

A.G.: Well, if the Kensho that is induced by the Yasutani Roshi method is not acknowledged by other Roshis, on what grounds is it not acknowledged?

HAMMER: I think the point just made was that it is understood that you have a psychological imposition in the method that is followed in America, where—I suppose they don't use this language—Satori becomes a kind of brainwashing operation.

Whereas the Zen Roshi here in Japan would want very violently to oppose any such notion that Satori comes simply from psychological motivation.

A.G.: The point may be a bit abstruse, but it interests me very much. It raises the questions, of course, What is the Enlightenment experience, and what is true Enlightenment? I'd love to hear any amount about that.

HAMMER: I think the very attempt to explain it also raises the questions what language you're going to use, and whether you're going to explain it in terms simply of psychological reactions, which is what Erich Fromm and others of the Jungian school would want to do. That's the attraction of Zen for some of your American psychologists—they're thinking of Satori largely in terms of psychological effect.

A.G.: Wouldn't they say that what Sakyamuni underwent was a psychological experience?

HAMMER: They probably would. But I think your Buddhists here in Japan would not want to bring the explanation of Sakyamuni's experience simply into the realm of psychology. They wouldn't want to turn religion into psychology. It's easier in talking about the Buddhist philosophy to say what it isn't rather than what it is.

A.G.: It's the same with the Christian philosophy. You use the phrase "Buddhist belief." What is the belief *in*, or what *is* the belief, in the case of Buddhism?

SAKAMOTO: We would rather refer to "faith" than to "belief."

A.G.: But doesn't "faith" have an object?

SAKAMOTO: The term "faith" is more frequently used in Pure Land Buddhism, especially Shin Buddhism, I think. And some Shin scholars or Shin adherents hold that the faith experience is equivalent to the Satori experience.

HAMMER: But it would be true, would it not, Sensei, to say that in both Zen and the Pure Land tradition you have the element of commitment? In the Satori experience you *commit* yourself to the experience. There is this parallel.

SAKAMOTO: Yes, your comment is acceptable to me.

A.G.: Do you think there's anything in this: if we were sufficiently enlightened, our response to reality wouldn't require any faith? As I understand it, there's no mystery about Buddhism. Faith comes into Christianity because of unseen elements and mysteries, to some extent. But as I understand it, that doesn't hold true with Buddhism. It is a response to the situation as seen, as experienced, and doesn't posit anything. Am I quite right about that?

SAKAMOTO: The Buddhist concept of faith is a little different. In Buddhism, faith is not merely intellectual. It moves man to the Bodhisattva way of life. There is something unconditional in "faith," but not in "belief."

HAMMER: I think Professor Abe said just before that it is important here in Japan to get a well-rounded understanding of what Japanese Buddhism means. And certainly in the Shingon tradition, the Esoteric tradition of Buddhism, you have a great amount of mystery, a great consciousness of mystery.

ABE: Yes, it's true. In the history of Japanese Buddhism, which includes not only Zen, but Pure Land and Esoteric Buddhism, mystery plays a very important part. It is a historical element and also an element that is still working in Japanese Buddhism. However, there is another question, another matter. What form of Buddhism most works . . .

A.G.: Is the most authentic, would you say?

ABE: *Really works* as the religious principle for modern man—for the contemporary and future world? This is another matter. What I said is the historical fact, but what I'm now talking about is the problem of value, evaluation. Which form of Buddhism or which form of religion?

A.G.: And that is the question that interests *me* most.

HAMMER: Is your criterion, then, utilitarian, or what? In your evaluation you say, "What really works?" Does this mean that your criterion is pragmatic? Or is it utilitarian? Or what is the criterion?

ABE: My criterion is how thoroughly the religion in question can solve the fundamental problems inherent in human existence. That is my criterion. Father Graham raised the question "What is the true nature of religion?" I think this may be related to the same point that I am talking about. In my view, dialogue between religions *today* should not be concerned merely with the comparison of two religions in their existing forms, but with which form of religion can really solve the fundamental problems of human existence. From that viewpoint Buddhism and Christianity should be examined.

SAKAMOTO: I would like to put Professor Abe's contention in another way. In Buddhism, especially in Japanese Buddhism, the problem of the adequacy of teaching to time and human situation or existential situation is a very important problem. From this point of view the true religion, to which someone makes a decision or commitment, is a religion that is truly adequate to time and the human existential situation. I think this is what Professor Abe means. Then, I would like to call the criterion "existential" rather than "pragmatic."

A.G.:   I suggest for consideration the thought that, so far as the West is concerned, and possibly Japan also, what seems to be the contemporary religious requirement is that what is presented for acceptance be in terms of evidence, evidence parallel in some way to scientific evidence, and also in terms of experience, so that an individual *feels* in some way, not only knows, but knows and feels, that the situation makes sense. So there would be generated an existential compassion, which does not seem to result from ideologies or doctrinal commitments in any notable degree today. That is why the Buddhist, and specifically the Zen, insight interests me so much—because it seems to require the minimum in terms of acceptance of mystery and to produce a compassionate integrity which is very remarkable. I've seen evidence of it here in meeting distinguished Roshis round about Kyoto. It's that that interests me so much in terms of throwing more light on the Christian tradition and perhaps being a standpoint from which the Christian theologians can criticize their own situation.

DOI: According to the Thomistic tradition, much emphasis is put on the truth value of religion, meaning by "truth value" that it

must be knowledge of the ultimate reality. Your standpoint
sounds more existential, rather than Thomistic. Am I right?

A.G.:   I couldn't agree more, Professor, with your first statement
that the Thomistic, Saint Thomas's, approach is concerned with
truth value. That is why he describes God as V*eritas Prima*.
Saint Thomas is more interested in theology than he is in Chris-
tology, so he says that the object of faith is V*eritas prima*, first
truth. It's not faith in *Christ* for Saint Thomas, but faith in
V*eritas prima*, God as truth. Now I reject totally any antithesis
between truth and existentialism. One of the great Thomist authorities, Gilson, has pointed out that Thomas Aquinas, of all
theologians, is the most existentialist, that he is concerned not so
much with the noun as with the verb, not so much with *essentia*
as with *esse* and the actual existential being, and of course with
truth in action. But that's a very big topic, so let's leave it that
way.

ABE: What is essential in Buddhism, particularly in Zen, is not to
believe in, or to have faith in, ultimate reality, God, whatever
you call it, but self-realization of reality or self-awakening of
ultimate reality. Because reality or ultimate reality is not something as object of faith or belief, nor is it something that stands
against us in the sense of immanence or transcendence. But we
are *in* reality, we are a manifestation of reality itself. So, this is
called self-realization; self-realization of *reality*. On the one
hand, one realizes reality, the ultimate basis of the world; on the
other hand, this means self-manifestation of reality through him.
So self-realization, in the Buddhist sense, particularly in the Zen
sense, means no difference between the realizer and what is realized, while in terms of faith or belief there is always the object of
faith and the subject of faith. This may be the essential difference between Buddhism and religions of faith.

A.G.:   That's how I would understand it.

HAMMER: Professor Abe, you've sometimes used the word "Buddhism," but you're really meaning here strictly the Zen understanding of Buddhism. Because if you were thinking of, say,
Jodo, Jodo-shin-shu, you could only reach your kind of explana-

tion if you said that the notion of commitment to an object in Jodo is a temporary Hoben and is not part of the ultimate truth involved.

ABE: I mean by the term "Buddhism" the original form propounded by Sakyamuni himself. I understand that Zen takes this original standpoint of Sakyamuni in its purest and most thoroughgoing way.

HAMMER: Except that, Sensei, you used a phrase, "We are a manifestation of reality." That sentence would seem to go contrary to Genshi-Bukkyo, original Buddhism, because the very Anatta theory means that you cannot talk about "we," you cannot say "we" or "I" at all. Now when you use that kind of language, you're just using it for the moment, are you?

ABE: If I state that he is not a manifestation of reality, he must be said to be in *avidya*, that is, ignorance. In reality we *are* in reality, and we are at least a part of reality.

A.G.: Well, who is the "we" in that case?

HAMMER: Yes, this is my problem. The recognition of a part of the whole would seem to give you pluralism over against monism.

ABE: "We" means you or I or anyone.

HAMMER: Yes, here you are using what I would call ordinary common-sense language, but is it legitimate to use common-sense language of this kind in describing reality in a Buddhist context? This is my question. You see, I'm really wanting to know whether you are really describing Buddhism as the Buddhist tradition would want Buddhism to be described, or whether you yourself are influenced through your study of other religions and other philosophies and are using the language that, say, I as a Christian might use to explain Christian experiences.

ABE: I'm trying to express the Buddhist idea, perhaps not necessarily in historical Christian terms. But I think if you say that we should not be said to be a manifestation of reality, where do we find ourselves?

HAMMER: This is Father Graham's point: what do you mean by "we," you see? I think we've had the question before: What is religion? We've also had the nature of the Satori experience. You really come back to this point: if we understand what we mean by man in the first place, we shall probably then be at the point of saying what we mean about religion, or about religious experience at the same time. Professor Ramsey, who is now Bishop of Durham, deals with the problem of "I," the problem of first-person sentences, in one of his books. Any existential language, too, tends to come back to this problem of the "I," whether this kind of language really can go along with the denial of the I, whether a true Anatta doctrine can be expressed in existential language at all.

DOI: Professor Abe, you don't distinguish between two levels of reality, two dimensions of reality?

ABE: Not two levels or dimensions of reality.

DOI: I mean the existential level of reality and the *essential* level of reality. In the existential level we feel the ultimate reality as "the other." This is the very starting point of religious aspiration, isn't it? Without this sense of otherness no religious aspiration can start.

ABE: That understanding is different from the Zen position. If you understand reality as something other, that realization cannot be called self-realization, but may be said to be faith or belief or something like that. So, what is most essential in the original form of Buddhism, and particularly in Zen, is not faith or belief, but self-realization, self-awakening to reality as such. The ultimate reality is not something other than the realizer. The realizer does not stand outside the reality, but may be said to be at least a part of that reality. So I said that he is a self-manifestation of reality as such. This realization—that one is the self-manifestation of ultimate reality as such—is *his* realization.

HAMMER: But at this point you are beyond language and you are beyond what you would call knowledge or thought, because language, knowledge, or thought *involves* this activity of objectification. And you cannot *express* anything without this element of the expresser sitting in judgment on that which is being expressed or having the object of his statement over against him.

K

You are saying for the moment, then, are you, as Professor Doi suggested, that you are in a sense speaking on two levels? On the first level, you *are* using the language of the part and the whole and you are regarding yourself as a bit of the total reality, and you say that fundamentally there can be no differentiation between the part and the whole. But once you state that the subject and the object are completely identified, which of course you have in the original Hindu tradition as well, then you get to the point where nothing can be said or related or interpreted. Now is not this, to come back to Father Graham's original point, part of the very problem of Zen and the understanding of Zen in Europe and America—that here you would say that *any* interpretation is a kind of preliminary, in a sense getting *into* the subject? Once you are *at* Satori, Satori is not solely self-expression or solely self-realization, because that is thinking of it psychologically and that is *still* differentiating one self from the totality. But, rather, the Satori must then be at the point where you are *beyond* speech or *beyond* interpretation, because there is the complete identification of the realizer and the reality that is realized. Would you say that this is part of the difficulty in the understanding of Zen in the West? That the West would still want to have the continuing dichotomy between the realizer and that which is realized? And therefore the understanding of Zen would be largely in terms of a psychological self-realization.

DOI: In Christianity, even after the unity between the ultimate reality and the self is achieved, otherness does not disappear; otherness remains; otherwise there can be no progress in our life. But in Zen Buddhism, after the Enlightenment, identity between the true self and the existential self is achieved: there can be no sense of otherness. Is that the Zen position?

A.G.:   Just to interpose for a minute: in the ultimate Christian experience as described by Christian mystics like Eckhart or John of Ruysbroeck, I don't gather that there is much sense of otherness. I think in the traditional Christian categories the sense of otherness is profound because of our inheritance from the Old Testament and partly from the New Testament. But I wonder to what extent that sense of otherness represents the *full* Christian tradition? It represents the *transcendence* of God, of course, but complementing that, in the very center of the Catholic tradition, is the immanence of God. So I just throw the question out from the Christian point of view: Even at the deeply religious level, how ultimate is the sense of otherness? Isn't the sense of self-*loss* even more ultimate—he who loses his life will find it? That, perhaps, might be the ultimate category, when you're not thinking in terms of I and Thou at all—that's a much publicized book, but I don't find it satisfying. With regard to what Professor Abe has been saying, with which I find myself, so far as I understand it, in very considerable agreement, I wonder if he would say that from the Buddhist point of view the *self* as sensed over against something else is an illusion, one of the illusions that we have to get rid of. And that in Buddhist terminology it's the collection of the skandhas that we find so troublesome. We have to use the language "I," "we," and "you" for conventional purposes in the actual world, but ultimately there's some getting beyond that, and that is what self-realization is. So I've raised two points, really, one for Professor Doi and one for Professor Abe.

VAN BRAGT: On the position of mysticism and Christianity: in Japan, they always seem to conclude that there is an opposition between Christian mysticism and theology.

HAMMER: I don't think so. Between *some* forms of mysticism.

VAN BRAGT: Yes. I want to ask Father Graham if he could comment a little bit on the position of mysticism in Christianity. It's often said in Japan that Eckhart and other people are more at home in Buddhism than in Christianity.

A.G.:   There is quite a big story. I suppose the word "mysticism" goes back to Greek theology, or to the Eleusinian mysteries, the revealing of something hidden. In the Christian tradition, there have been certain confrontations between mystics, like Eckhart, for instance, and the theologians. But Aldous Huxley made a good point in that connection: that a pious fraud had been perpetrated, namely the appearance of certain writings under the name of Dionysius the Areopagite. The alleged author wrote a treatise called *Mystical Theology*. He was supposed to have been a disciple of Saint Paul, so even the canon lawyers, the legalists, people for whom mysticism was more or less a closed book, couldn't oppose a life, an activity, that was sanctioned by apostolic or sub-apostolic authority. Whereas it was discovered, as we know now, that Dionysius the Areopagite wasn't a Christian at all—barely one—but was a neo-Platonist philosopher, a Syrian monk. I think it's wrong to say he was not a Christian, but he was not sanctioned by apostolic authority. It seems to me that in the Catholic tradition the mystics and the theologians have got along pretty well together. The thing was analyzed, again by Thomas Aquinas, who was himself a mystic. When he had his mystical experience, he followed the Zen pattern—he didn't write any more; he was silent; he didn't try to ratiocinate after he'd had his Enlightenment experience. But he knew something of that experience, and he analyzed it in terms of a quasi experience of God. He quoted Dionysius the Areopagite that not only do you have to do the will of God, but you have to be *patiens divina*, you have to suffer, experience, feel the divinity or divine things. That is usually what is understood in orthodox Catholic circles by "mystical experience"—a kind of *feeling*, a sense of what they call "the Divine," which perhaps in Buddhist terminology is called "self-realization." There have been some conflicts, but I can't think of any notable conflict. John of the Cross, for instance, was one of the greatest mystics, and he worked it out quite satisfactorily within orthodox terminology. Of course it's open for anybody to say from the Buddhist tradition that those were conceptualizations and that conceptual framework was very much in terms of the distinction between I and Thou. But the basic experience, the mystical experience, was there in the Christian tradition and not disapproved of, although perhaps it was very seldom understood by the ordinary run-of-the-mill canonists and bishops, the people who ran the ecclesiastical machinery. I'm not too happy, incidentally, with the linking together of the Zen experience of Enlightenment with Catholic mysticism. I don't follow that myself. As I understand it, the Catholic mystical experience is the *culmination* of devotional life, of bhakti, and extremely religious, rather in terms of I and Thou. It is very ethereal and otherworldly for the most part. Whereas my understanding of the Zen experience is that it's very down-to-earth, very matter-of-fact, a very *with-it* experience. So I feel that a good deal of thought has to be given to that before people rather glibly bring together Catholic mysticism and the Zen experience.

Conversation between Dr. William H. Collins and
Dom Aelred Graham in Kyoto, September 23, 1967.

A.G.: You must be very familiar now with the scene in Kyoto.

W.H.C.: The first year and a half I was here I didn't really make
much effort to learn the language; I hoped to get by without it.
But this seemed rather limiting to what one could achieve. Since
then I've been making a fairly steady attempt to learn the language.

A.G.: It's a difficult language, isn't it?

W.H.C.: Yes, it is, because it really has nothing in common with
European languages, so you've got to start from scratch.

A.G.: Are you now studying under some Zen Master?

W.H.C.: No, I'm not under any Zen Master at the moment. I find
that I can't do the long hours of sitting that they seem to require.

A.G.: You are a psychologist, aren't you? What do you feel the
value is from the psychological or psychiatric point of view?

W.H.C.: I think the position, the sitting position, is quite important, but not essential. I also think the group sitting that they go
in for, the usual thing here, is also helpful: you can make more
rapid progress than by sitting by yourself. However, I think you
can manage by sitting on your own. I must say that I've gotten

rather interested in the general psychology of the Japanese and where they get their energy.

A.G.: That would be interesting to hear about.

W.H.C: Of course I haven't solved that problem, but I think in some way their method of thinking is more haphazard than that of the West. They go more by their intuition. I think that uses up less nervous energy than the kind of thought that we go in for in the West.

H.T.: What have you thought about the "haphazard" way of thinking and how it uses up less energy?

W.H.C.: According to the general psychological theory, people use up much of their energy in repressing various desires and emotions rather than on any form of action. Thus, much of their nervous energy is used up in a purely negative way. I feel that with the Japanese much less energy is used up negatively in that way, that their spontaneous thoughts and feelings get more expression.

A.G.: Are you a practicing psychologist or psychiatrist here in Kyoto?

W.H.C.: No. I can't very well practice, because I'd have to pass a medical examination in Japanese before I was allowed to practice in this country.

A.G.: Have you come to any tentative views or conclusions or over-all picture of the Buddhist scene in Japan?

W.H.C.: I have formed certain conclusions. On the whole, Buddhism is not in a very healthy state here. The two chief forms of Buddhism, the Shin and Zen schools, are divided. Shin, which is the most important, is divided into Jodo and the Jodo-shin-shu, which is the larger sect; and Zen is divided into the Soto and Rinzai. Soto is much the larger sect, and as a popular religion I think it has much more to offer than Rinzai. The chief fault in Buddhism, in my opinion, is not the basic substance of the religion, which I think is really pretty sound in its tenets, but the obsession with the negative statement. They won't say what a thing is; they'll only say what it is not. That really may be more accurate in describing metaphysical realities, but there does come a time when I feel it's self-defeating. People want a positive answer to some ultimate questions, even if it is in some way inaccurate. All through the language here you see this negative way of putting things. They much prefer to ask a negative question rather than a positive one. For instance, they say, "It isn't so, is it?" instead of "Is a thing so?"

H.T.: What interested you originally about Buddhism? It seems to me that negative statement is integral to Buddhism, whereas if one is concerned with having a positive statement about metaphysical realities, it would seem that Christianity offers that.

W.H.C.: What interested me about Buddhism was that the Buddha seemed to be rather like a physician, in the way he'd go about investigating and treating a case of illness—illness of a spiritual nature. So because of my medical background, I suppose, the Buddhist approach appealed to me and seemed eminently reasonable.

A.G.: Was there anything in particular that prompted you to want to have a talk with me? Is it anything I said or is it just in general?

W.H.C.: It's in general, really, but what I did notice at your talk was that you didn't offer any negative criticism of Buddhism or Buddhism in Japan.

A.G.: I'd love to hear what your criticism is.

W.H.C.: There is the problem I've already mentioned of Buddhism being too negative in its exposition, which for the man in the street is rather unsatisfactory, I feel. I think the Chinese and the Japanese have never taken too kindly to Buddhism, not in the same way that India and Southeast Asia accepted it. Of course, afterward it died out in India, and I think it was partly because they got fed up with this negative way of putting things, and Sankara came along and stated things rather better.

A.G.: Wouldn't they say, the apologists for Buddhism in this country, particularly of the Zen school, that it's not that they're negative in essence, but that they're negative in expression because they want to eliminate conceptual thinking and verbalizations and concentrate on the experience of what reality is, what

Enlightenment is? And since that cannot be expressed in conceptual terms, to which the West is wedded, it appears to a Westerner negative, but in fact is trying to establish something quite positive. Wouldn't they say something like that, perhaps?

w.h.c.: Yes, I suppose they would if they could. Of course the trouble with so many of the Zen authorities here, and I think it applies to Japanese on the whole, is that they're not good at conceptual thinking; they can't express themselves. They can only say, "If you want to know about Zen, do as I do." They can't explain what Zen is. Western religious teachers, and I think this applies to Indian ones as well, may finally come down to saying that you've got to put the thing into practice, but they, at any rate, can give a reasonable intellectual exposition, which a Westerner usually expects before he starts any new venture. On the whole he doesn't think much of blindly following somebody's example.

a.g.: Before coming to the Buddhist scene, you must have been interested in what the Enlightenment, or Satori, experience is or amounts to from a psychological point of view. Do you feel you could say anything about that, perhaps in positive terms?

w.h.c.: When you read about the experience of mystics of any religious background, you're surprised to find how much in common there seems to be in the experiences, although they are to such a large degree ineffable. So that one feels that there's really nothing particularly unique about the Zen Satori experience.

a.g.: Buddhists wouldn't think of Enlightenment in terms of a union with a transcendental deity, would they, in the way that Christians and Muslims are apt to do?

w.h.c.: I don't think so. I don't know to what extent it's true that they believe in a sort of higher self. I know that the Shin Buddhists definitely believe that Amida Buddha is essentially the higher self that they desire to merge with. But I think the Zen people are very chary of believing that there is any entity that can be regarded as a being that they merge with. I think if they do put it into words, it would be something like realizing that samsara is identical with nirvana.

A.G.: I understand that there's a controversy going on within the Zen school itself about what Satori is and how it's to be achieved. Would you know anything about that?

W.H.C.: I know that the view of the Soto people is that Satori is *already* achieved, that it's just a question of being patient and doing your sitting and your other duties in life and you'll gradually realize it. But you're not to go searching about for something that you believe you haven't got. In that way there's a slight difference between the Soto and the Rinzai. The Rinzai people seem to be definitely searching for something that they haven't got; but the Soto people are always trying to play that down. They're less showy and spectacular than the Rinzai people.

A.G.: In what way do the Rinzai people get spectacular, would you say?

W.H.C.: They have an elaborate battery of koans, and there are witty dialogues between masters and monks.

A.G.: And they beat people up, I understand, to get them . . .

W.H.C.: Yes. Of course it's not all one way, you know; occasionally it's the pupil who beats up the master. But that's carefully expunged from the record.

A.G.: As a psychologist, what do you think about all that?

W.H.C.: It tends to bring about some very undesirable exhibitionism.

A.G.: I would think so.

W.H.C.: I've done some sitting at various times with groups of people, and they occasionally used to shout and grunt during the sitting. I felt that that wasn't really some "other power," but that it was definitely "self-power." But there again, of course, that's one of the Japanese characteristics, that before they work themselves up into a real pitch of energy and activity, they like to do various noisy things, either shouting or playing. For instance, they like military bands in this country. And one way or another they like to shout and grunt.

A.G.: Like the Italians—the military bands!

W.H.C.: Same as the New Zealand Maoris—that war dance before the warriors went into action. I think quite a proportion of the

Japanese did come from the South Sea Islands; you can see it in the architecture of the houses. It's a South Sea look much more suitable for hot weather than cold. But the fact is that quiet enthusiasm is something that isn't so common in this country as it is in the West. They feel much better if they can make shouts and grunts and noises before they get down to work. Before the summer vacation there was a student who every night about midnight used to go just outside the temple and make grunts and noises and count one, two, three, four, five. Then he'd give a grunt and start again. It used to get on my nerves. No doubt he was getting ready for some important event or trial of strength.

A.G.:   Kensho, don't they call it? The big event?

W.H.C.:   Yes, an important spiritual experience.

A.G.:   Well, I've just been reading a book by a man named Philip Kapleau, who's a Westerner.

W.H.C.:   Yes, I've heard of him.

A.G.:   He takes all those aspects of the matter terribly seriously, the grunting and the noise and the beatings and so on—they're all part of the *mise en scène*—very important, apparently.

W.H.C.:   Well I think in certain circumstances it can be the right thing. But, as I say, there is a tendency for an unhealthy exhibitionism to creep in. I've made some criticisms regarding Buddhism, and now I'd like to make a criticism of Zen. And that is a sort of lack of *metta*, good will and loving-kindness.

A.G.:   Compassion.

W.H.C.:   Yes, compassion.

A.G.:   That's my impression, yes.

W.H.C.:   This lack very much slows up the enlightening process. I feel if there was really warmth and good will for one's fellow men, if that was encouraged more, the enlightening process would go on a lot quicker.

A.G.:   I think that's a very shrewd observation.

W.H.C.:   Because this basic void or emptiness that the Mahayana believe in is supposed to have two elements. Wisdom is one and compassion is the other.

A.G.:   *Prajna* and *karuna*, that's right.

w.h.c.: But the *karuna* seems to be very much left out in the Zen training.

a.g.: I suppose they would say that if you were sufficiently enlightened, compassion, *karuna*, would follow. But they don't seem to stress it. For instance, I was just noticing in the book *The Three Pillars of Zen* that what the author stresses, as does Yasutani Roshi, on whose teaching the book is based, is that if you get the Zen insight, it will enable you to meet all the difficulties of life—say, the atomic bomb—with dignity and composure. Well, I would have thought that perhaps a little more was required, that perhaps if you had sufficient compassion you might try to do something about stopping the atomic bomb from falling.

w.h.c.: Yes, I think it is possible to attain Enlightenment along Zen lines, but it is very much slowed up by neglecting the compassionate side of the spirit.

a.g.: I think that's interesting and important. Have you had much contact with Zen personalities, Zen authorities, Roshis and so on?

w.h.c.: To some extent, yes. I've had one or two talks with Yamada Mumon Roshi. I think he's one of the best Roshis at the present time. He is a very kindly man. I think he does understand the importance of compassion himself. He's also one of the few Zen authorities who can express himself. Although he hasn't got much knowledge of English, he's a very eloquent speaker in Japanese apparently. I have a rather high opinion of him. And I have met other Roshis. Nakagawa Soen Roshi has a good knowledge of English. I believe he's a very competent Roshi, too.

a.g.: My difficulty with the Roshis would be, if, *per impossible*, I were not already committed to another tradition, to ascribe to them the kind of infallibility of insight that the true disciples are supposed to, so that the Roshi seems to know precisely what's what and can discern without hesitation, immediately and without possibility of error, when somebody has become enlightened.

w.h.c.: There seem to be degrees in the amount of authority that is attributed to the Roshi. Somebody like Dr. Schloegel could give you better information on that, I think, because she worked intimately under a very good Roshi.

h.t.: Who is her Roshi?

w.h.c.: Oda Roshi. He died last autumn.

h.t.: Oh, yes. He was head of Daitoku-ji? She seems sold on the Roshi-disciple relationship.

w.h.c.: Yes, but she's not so completely sold as some people. An acquaintance studied under the Soto tradition at Soji-ji at Yokohama. Here the disciple seemed bound hand and foot to the Roshi in a closer relationship than is usual with the Rinzai training. But the relationships may vary, nevertheless. I think Dr. Schloegel has kept a degree of independence. But isn't there, under any religious discipline, a tendency to come completely under the influence of the teacher?

a.g.: I don't know that that's true in the Christian West, at least in the Catholic tradition, and I would doubt it very much in the Protestant tradition. I think that there is a general body of doctrine that is accepted and understood, of course in general terms, and there is the appeal to the Bible and tradition and the general authority of the church. That gives an over-all cover or arch or dome, or whatever phrase one cares to use about an authoritative framework. But I don't think that the individual priest or even a spiritual director is taken with anything like the seriousness or given anything like the authority that Zen students and disciples seem to give to the Roshi. This is because the assumption in Christianity and in Catholicism is that the individual conscience is in some way, however obscurely, in direct contact with God, the Holy Spirit of Truth. So the ultimate court of appeal is one's own conscience, the "still small voice within," and even a convert to the Roman Church like John Henry Newman could make his famous toast "I toast my conscience first and the Pope afterwards." So antecedently, a person like myself would tend to have considerable reservations.

w.h.c.: Personally I find it very difficult to accept the absolute authority of a Roshi. Of course they have the same idea in India with the guru. But I've talked to Indians about it, and they say that's not suitable for everybody; there are people who are so constituted that it's not the right thing for them to have a guru. They may have something in the nature of a spiritual guru, some saint who is long since dead, but not a living human being. It's not always essential to their Enlightenment to have a living guru.

A.G.: Is that the Indian view?

W.H.C.: That's a view that I was told in India.

A.G.: I have sympathy with that. My feeling is, just to use an ethical category for a moment, without evaluating it or getting hung up on it, that it's not so much that it's bad for the student or the disciple to be hung up on a guru or a Roshi, but it's bad for the Roshi or the guru to feel that he has that kind of power. It seems to me that ultimately a guru or a Roshi has his authority not just because he has some official status, but because of his greater experience and insight. And the test of his value is to what extent what he says commends itself intrinsically to the student or disciple. So that a disciple or student can say, "Oh, yes, I see that: that makes sense," rather than, "That's what you say, and I go along with that because you say it."

W.H.C.: Treating the Roshi as though he were a god is really a sort of childish attitude, isn't it? It's not the attitude of a grown-up person. I wonder if you've met Suzuki Roshi?

A.G.: He has founded a monastery in Tassajara, outside San Francisco. Yes, I've met him.

W.H.C.: He was here in Japan last summer, and I met him. I was rather impressed by him, as most people are. I think he's a very sound man indeed.

A.G.: He seems to be.

W.H.C.: But I wanted to mention the aspect of *metta*, loving-kindness, in relation to Zen meditation. You know in Tibet they have a form of meditation in which they generate quite a lot of physical heat. Of course it's very useful in a cold climate, and it would be very useful here in Japan, because some of these temples and monasteries get bitterly cold in the winter. But in Japan they haven't got anything like that; they just have to bear the cold stoically. I think the reason that this psychic method of generating physical heat is not practiced in this country is that although it's partly a matter of breath control, it's also to a large extent the generation of a really strong feeling of good will to all sentient beings. And that's something that they don't seem to have here. On the other hand, the Japanese are emotionally very sensitive and subtle.

A.G.: Apropos of that, I get the impression, after two months in Japan, of great amiability, even toward Westerners, on the people's part. The Zen people do, of course, don't they, take the vow and renew the vow to save all sentient beings at the end of their Zen sessions? That's my observation of it. I've also noticed that their dogs look very well cared for, very cheerful, rather different from the average run of dogs in the West. We went out to Nara the other day and saw those deer in the park coming up to be fed, which you would never find in a park in America or in England. Isn't that right?

W.H.C.: I think they're somewhat ambivalent toward animals in this country. They don't really understand dogs. They feed them quite well and they brush them, but they don't understand that the dog's a very active animal that needs plenty of exercise. But then, of course, if they think that it is essential that the animal have exercise, they tow them around by motorbicycle.

H.T.: A view of the Japanese mentality is beginning to emerge.

A.G.: Was your own background in Guernsey, in the West, Christian, more or less?

W.H.C.: Yes. I was brought up an Anglican.

A.G.: Did you feel there was some deficiency there that led you to come out here? Didn't you feel that the Archbishop of Canterbury had the whole story?

W.H.C.: No. For a long time I felt somehow that it didn't appeal to the emotional side. However, I think the Church of England is a very English institution, that in some way it seems to mirror the English character to a large extent.

A.G.:   Wouldn't some people say that perhaps it's none the worse for being that?

W.H.C.:   Possibly.

A.G.:   But you mean it's rather insular and provincial?

W.H.C.:   It's rather phlegmatic and undemonstrative. However, I don't know to what extent I really am English, because three of my grandparents were Irish. I spent nine years in Ireland, actually. I did my medical training there. So I do understand the Catholic attitude to some extent. And also I've been quite interested in the Orthodox Church. Twice I've been to Athos, and also to the monastery of Laggovarda, on Paros. I think that's the older religion, and that the Reformation tended to throw out the baby with the bath water to some extent. If they couldn't find that something was definitely mentioned in the Bible, well then, it had to go. That was, I suppose, the view of Cranmer and his associates. But I think it's rather a pity myself. I can't see really that the Revelation came to an end with the Bible; surely it's continued in some way after that. There have been saints, and people surely have been inspired since then.

A.G.:   The Bible and the Bible only: that was more or less the Continental Reformers rather than the Anglican Church, wasn't it? They have *some* sense of church tradition.

W.H.C.:   Yes. But the question of the Mother of God was completely cut out. The work of Jung has shown that this element is really rather important, that it exists in man's unconscious and manifests itself in various ways, and it's only justifiable that it should be given scope. I've noticed in the Orthodox Church that the Ikon of the Mother of God seems to get more devotion than any other ikon. If that's taken away, it surely leaves a gap for many people in their religious life.

We're a little off the subject of Zen. I recently read quite an interesting book, recommended by the Bishop of Woolwich. It's a book called *Incognito*, by a Rumanian ex-Communist. I think it must be largely autobiographical. First it describes his early life. Then he got fed up with being at home, and at the beginning of the last war volunteered to fight against the Russians and had quite a distinguished record. He was eventually captured by the

Russians, fought for them, and was converted to Communism. Then for some years he had quite a promising career back in Rumania as a member of the Communist party. Then he gradually became disillusioned. He thought that although many of the Communist reforms were good, there was too much hatred mixed up in their attitude toward people who didn't fall into line. He gradually became more and more disillusioned, and finally he threw the whole thing up. That caused great offense, since he was a fairly important member of the party, and of course they were extremely unpleasant to him. He was thrown into prison and had very unpleasant experiences. With all the soldiering and campaigning, he had had a very hard time for most of his life. He had seen the very worst side of life. Then, suddenly, he realized that he'd never really tried to love the world; he'd always rather tended to be up against it. So he changed over to trying to love the world rather than hate it. He felt that all men were really aspects of God in some way and they were all to be loved, however difficult it was. It's a rather interesting book, I think, particularly on the topic of religious conversion.

H.T.: Petru Dumitriu, is it?

W.H.C.: Yes.

A.G.: My own feeling or thought is that religion has to work itself more and more along those lines, more and more in finding God in the human situation rather than in some transcendental realms.

W.H.C.: Would you feel that in religion the important thing is the religious experience itself rather than the search for any definite benefit in it, like the search for a heaven?

A.G.: I'd have to think that out before I could agree. I would think the test would be what that experience engendered. I would say that the Buddhist line there is the fruitful one; namely, in terms of wisdom and compassion. So that I think the value of religious experience is to be assessed by the quality of wisdom and compassion that results from it, or follows on it anyhow.

W.H.C.: Yes, that would be the test from the external and objec-

L

tive viewpoint. The wisdom and compassion would show the inner workings of the religious attitude.

A.G.:   I would think so, yes. Would you feel there was something in that?

W.H.C.:   I think that if the religious attitude was fruitful it would certainly result in an increase in wisdom and compassion.

A.G.:   What would you say the religious experience is? Seeing that you were keen on trying to find some positive way of expressing these things.

W.H.C.:   A feeling, I suppose, of infinite well-being. A feeling of oneness, of unity, and absence of ego-feeling, I think.

A.G.:   Yes, I think that's pretty good. A kind of selflessness and feeling that . . .

W.H.C.:   You might say you have the sea and the waves; that one starts off by being a wave and feeling that one's almost a separate entity as a wave, and then going from that to feel that though one's still a wave, one's essentially, more importantly, part of the ocean.

A.G.:   Yes. I think that's good.

W.H.C.:   There's something that I thought I might possibly ask you about the view of Christ's mission on earth. The Jews had an idea of the absolute transcendence of God, that there was a complete gulf between God and man, and what caused so much offense amongst the Jews was that he was breaching this gulf. I mean, he talked about his intimacy with the Father.

A.G.:   I think that's right, yes.

W.H.C.:   But then, of course, what he was by nature he said we could become, I think, by grace; that we could also become sons of God.

A.G.:   Yes. I think that's true and very much to the point and illuminating.

W.H.C.:   There's a tendency in Christianity to revert to the old Jewish idea.

A.G.:   The Judaic idea, that's right.

W.H.C.:   I think some of the Protestant churches rather go in for that.

A.G.: Yes, I think there is almost an unconscious tendency to promote that way of looking at things as soon as the church gets institutionalized, because the priesthood and the hierarchy must have some *raison d'être*. Therefore, they need to be intermediaries between man and God, and with God up above and man down below, they're rather nicely placed to act as mediators. That is something perhaps that needs to be exposed to criticism at this time.

W.H.C.: Why do you think that Christianity has made so little headway here in Japan? Apparently when it was first introduced, in the early days of the Shogunate, it made rather rapid progress. Then, unfortunately, it became politically suspect and was suppressed. Now it doesn't seem to make a lot of headway, yet I should have thought it was a religion that in many ways would appeal to the Japanese rather more than Buddhism does. It's more positive, and I think that appeals more to the Japanese in general.

A.G.: Wasn't it a happy accident, so far as you can use the word "accident," that when the first mission of Saint Francis Xavier arrived, they made a fortunate contact with the representatives of the Shogunate, who were on the outs with the Buddhists at the time, and that Christianity was a religion that supported the established order, was not critical of it, and believed in a hierarchy and God and so on? So the authorities gave it their patronage to begin with, as against the Buddhist indifference to this world and the institutions of this world. Also the Buddhist monks were rather troublesome I think. They had large property, and the Shogunate wanted to do something about that. As a counterweight to Buddhism, Christianity was perhaps disproportionately patronized by the authorities. That, I think, corresponds roughly to the historical situation when the Jesuits first arrived. Then the failure came because it was felt that these missionaries were representatives of foreign powers, that they were just representing Portugal or Spain, as the case might be. I don't know to what extent Christianity might be more congenial to the Japanese temperament than Buddhism. Looking around

these shrines and temples, I feel they are built much closer to
the natural scene of things than, say, the great Gothic spires or
Romanesque domes of Europe. Buddhism is more, perhaps, a
religion of nature, down-to-earth to a certain extent. Could that
be true? And it appeals to the artistic temperament. I think
Buddhist iconography is more pleasing than Christian on aesthetic grounds.

W.H.C.:   In Eastern Europe the Byzantine churches and architecture seem to fit very well into the natural setting. I thought the
spires of the Gothic churches seem to reach up to heaven, while
the Orthodox churches seem to cling to the earth rather like
limpets. They seem in a way to fit in very well with the natural
scenery. One notices that particularly in Athos. It's really a very
beautiful place. It's been called the Garden of Mary, which is a
very suitable name for it.

A.G.:   My views on all this are extremely tentative. I'm going on to
Bangkok, and I'll be interested to hear the Theravada critique of
the Mahayana. Then I'm going on to India to hear the Hindu
critique of Buddhism, to put it rather sharply. And then on farther west, to Iran. I'd like to look at the Sufi situation. And then
back through Greece and Athos. So I haven't got, as the young
people say nowadays, a hang-up on any of this. I'm very impressed by the temperament, I suppose; I'm very impressed by
the intuitive and intellectual side of Buddhism. It posits that the
basis of good will must be understanding and insight, and I
think Christianity perhaps has overlooked that a bit. I am sympathetic with the Zen disparagement of words and verbal formulas and so on, because I think Christians got very hung up on
words and formulas and ideologies. It is possibly apparent that I
am quite sympathetic to the situation, at least tentatively.

W.H.C.:   I think a lot of religious energy in Japan has gone into the
new religions. They've really borrowed quite a lot from Christianity, as well as Buddhism.

A.G.:   It's very kind of you to come along and offer these insights,
enlarging the horizon, because it's very important to see the various aspects of things. Fortunately, I haven't come with any sort

of thesis to establish, but just to find out what's going on, so far as possible. Except, I do have a predilection for Sakyamuni's approach to things. The question is how faithfully that is reflected here, because, as we all know, Buddhism came from India, then went through China, and then it came here. It's undergone two transformations at least, hasn't it?

W.H.C.: I know the view in Ceylon is that it simply isn't Buddhism, what there is here. Of course, the Thais are rather more tolerant than the Sinhalese. They're in a position of rather more strength, Buddhism being strong in Thailand. They feel fairly sure of their ground, I think.

A.G.: I hope to have an opportunity to see something of these new religions—though my understanding is that insofar as they are *new* they reflect largely the peculiarly Japanese scene. Many of them owe much to Buddhism, which some of them—Soka Gakkai, for example—have perverted. My interest is in the true nature of the Buddhist message and its possible relation to Christianity.

Conversation between the Reverend Kaneko,
of Higashi Hongan-ji, the headquarters of the
Jodo-shin-shu, True Pure Land sect, of Buddhism,
and Dom Aelred Graham in Kyoto,
September 27, 1967.

The Reverend Shojun Bando translated.

A.G.:   I have come to Japan to learn about Buddhism, to understand it as much as possible and to see it in practice. Usually
Christians come to Japan to be missionaries; I have come to
learn and not to teach. While I was living in America, the form
of Buddhism I knew or learned most about was Zen. But I've
discovered here in Japan that the whole field of Buddhism is
much wider than that, and I'd very much like to hear the Buddhist emphasis that you think most important.

R.K.:   Here in Japan there are many important factors in Japanese
Buddhism, but I would like to mention three. The first is Zen;
the second is the Nembutsu of Pure Land Buddhism, which is
ordinarily considered to be quite the opposite of Zen; and the
third is Shingon, Esoteric Buddhism, including the so-called
Nichiren schools. These may be considered representative of
Japanese Buddhism. The central factor in the doctrine of Shingon
Buddhism is prayer; of Pure Land, recitation of Nembutsu (*Namu
Amida Butsu*—I find myself in Amida Buddha); of Zen, sitting
in meditation.

A.G.:   When you speak of prayer, who or what is it one prays to,
and what is the purpose of the prayer?

R.K.: I simply used the term "prayer." But in Shingon Buddhism technically prayer is expressed as *"kaji."* *"Ka"* means "adding"—adding of power by Vairocana, or Dainichi, the Shingon deity. His power is added or given to the devotees, so *kaji* expresses the interrelationship between Vairocana and the Shingon devotees from the viewpoint of the Buddha. But usually another term is added to *kaji,* which is *"kito."* The devotees receive the power from the Vairocana Buddha, so *kito* is prayer expressed from the viewpoint of the devotees to Vairocana Buddha.

A.G.: Prayer has the effect of helping the devotee along toward Enlightenment, is that right?

R.K.: It is not my purpose to explain Shingon Buddhism, but it is my general impression, which I have had since my childhood, that Shingon, of all schools in Japanese Buddhism, is very similar to Christianity. I said "devotees," but it should be rather, "practitioners." In the case of Shingon Buddhism practitioners, called *acarya*, are supposed to be intermediaries between devotees and Vairocana Buddha. So in Shingon Buddhism ultimate reality is supposed to be Vairocana Buddha, but in the general conception, he who saves people is that intermediary, called *acarya*. So in that sense, having the intermediary, it is my impression that Shingon and Christianity are similar. But the main differences may be these facts. First, Shingon gives you the impression that it is pantheistic or pluralistic, but Christianity does not. Then, the emphasis on salvation in this world is characteristic of Shingon Buddhism. This is greatly in contrast with other sects, Zen and Pure Land. Although Zen teaches Enlightenment, there is more emphasis in Zen on transcendence, attaining Enlightenment by transcending this world. In Zen and Pure Land Buddhism the impermanence of life and the problems of life and death are the main questions taken up. So these sects can be said to be rather subjective. Also, in Pure Land Buddhism especially, the thesis that life is suffering is very much emphasized. But in Shingon Buddhism it is not so; it is much more optimistic. So it is my impression that Kobo Daishi, the founder of Shingon Buddhism, and Nichiren Shonin, the founder of Nichiren Buddhism, lack the sense of impermanence. Their strong feeling is that one must save the world; all people in the world must be saved. That sense is much stronger than in Pure Land Buddhism.

A.G.: Apart from touching on the various sects or views, what do you yourself think is most important for a Westerner to know about Zen in general? I'm particularly interested in your view about what Enlightenment is and when it is attained? Is it attained in this world or in some other world; is it attained suddenly or gradually?

R.K.: Enlightenment is one with truth—*satya*, in Sanskrit. Satori is identical with *satya*, truth, ultimate truth, but in plain terms it means to see life clearly or to see things as they are. But there are problems: how can we see things clearly or how can we view life as it is; from where can we see life clearly; where is Enlightenment, outside us or inside us? The ultimate meaning of Satori may be that the ordinary eye becomes the enlightened eye, the eye that sees the world as it is and can view this life from the transcendent viewpoint. And in order to develop the eye that can see life as it is, practice or discipline is needed. Zen Buddhism says it is possible for us to reach this standpoint, which it calls the position of no position, in this world—not some other position from where we stand. The main difference between Pure Land Buddhism and Zen is that in Pure Land these two standpoints are not readily identified. Pure Land recognizes the clear or sharp difference between the present state and the state to be attained, and emphasizes the difference between them. In Zen Buddhism it can easily be identified; in Pure Land Buddhism it is said that it cannot easily be dissolved. In Dogen's Zen Buddhism the answer is given to the question of where the attainment is. It is said to be in the process of the discipline itself—not after we are enlightened, but in the process, there is Enlightenment; not after we have completed the discipline, but in the midst of the discipline, Enlightenment appears.

A.G.: Are there degrees of Enlightenment? Does it happen gradually or suddenly?

R.K.: Enlightenment is attained suddenly, but we should not be attached to the position of Enlightenment. In the process of our discipline Enlightenment appears, but after Enlightenment there are long stages to be covered. The teaching is "Don't be settled in one position." If one stops working, then the faith is dead. In order to go on infinitely, we should not be attached to the principle of Enlightenment after attaining it suddenly.

A.G.: I think I understand. One of the Christian saints, Saint Bernard, said, "If you do not move forward in the spiritual life, you move backward." Is that the same thing?

R.K.: Most probably so. A certain awareness suddenly dawns on one; then his course is suddenly changed. But, in the case of the ordinary man, he can regress and turn to some other way. So in order to warn the devotee of that danger, such a teaching might have been expressed. The reason why I say "most probably so" is to acknowledge my ignorance of the teaching of Christianity. I cannot say definitely "yes."

A.G.: Can the individual tell when he himself has been enlightened?

R.K.: Many factors can be pointed out, but one of the things that can be pointed to definitely is that one who is enlightened is able to see things with understanding. Formerly he saw things in a bad way; but after attaining awareness he can see things sympathetically or in the most favorable way. A certain thing may have been a hindrance or something that threatened him or which gave him only inconvenience, but now his nature is changed and he can interpret things in the most constructive and understanding way.

A.G.: That is very persuasive. It seems to me a much more modest presentation of Enlightenment than the Zen Satori, which is supposed to be a tremendous experience. According to the Zen tradition, the Roshi is supposed to be able to say in a moment whether somebody else, the disciple, is enlightened or not. Is that true of other sects as well?

R.K.: In order to have an insight you need practice, but it is true in Pure Land Buddhism that Enlightenment can be detected in another whether one is enlightened or not. Here is an example. There was a man who was very upright and honest and very well mannered, but visitors used to feel awkward and ill at ease in his presence. After he reached Enlightenment, his manner didn't change at all, because it was his custom since his childhood, but his visitors were now very much at ease. Why? Because the inner change made the guests feel more at ease. To have insight into other people one does not have to be a leader in religion. Ordinary people can detect what has happened.

A.G.: That is the same in Christianity. Often it is not the popes and bishops who have insight, but quite simple laymen. To go deeper into the philosophical foundation of all this, there's a famous Buddhist saying that lingers in my mind: "All in one and one in all." I wonder if you could comment on that to make it more intelligible, or less unintelligible?

R.K.: I understand it as an expression of the real understanding between man and man, or the understanding between people. It is the relationship between one and all others. On this spiritual level there is no gap, no disparity, no difference between one and others; it is the level on which all people can stand equally on the same footing. For example, it is an insight by which one can see oneself in the behavior or the spiritual life of others, and if one has an insight like this, then the human passions, love and hate, are not only the problems of other people, but of oneself. Whatever is existent in one can be found in others and vice versa. If such a new horizon dawns upon one, there is true harmony, there is true peace, there is true understanding between peoples. In that way I understand this philosophy.

A.G.: So that it's a human, psychological thing, not a metaphysical, ontological theory. I tried to put down in writing my understanding of the Satori experience. It would take me a few minutes and be a bit difficult to translate, but if you have time, I'd like to state it as I see it and ask you what you think about it. By way of prelude, my book *Zen Catholicism,* in which I stated my understanding of Satori, was reviewed in *Young East* by Philip Kapleau, who said that I didn't have the slightest idea what Satori was and that it didn't agree with the doctrine of Yasutani Roshi. On the other hand, an English Buddhist wrote to say that I understood the matter better than a great many Buddhists. What I now say is merely an expression of Western philosophy, the tradition of Plato, Aristotle, Thomas Aquinas . . .

R.K.: He has much to say! In order to perfect any practice, seemingly useless experience must be undergone. Any disciple who has entered any kind of practice must begin with seemingly unnecessary, futile things. But of course all these things are a part of the discipline. Without such seemingly trifling things there can be no perfecting of the practice. As to the recognition of the attainment, two aspects should be mentioned: one is recognition by the authentic master, and the second is recognition by the amateurish, unknowing, and unlearned masses. These two kinds of recognition seem to make up the recognition of the attainment of the practice, whatever it is, but so long as there is an attachment to the accomplishment, it is very doubtful whether it is genuine or not. As to Philip Kapleau's comment on your book, two things may be said. One is that he may be justified in view of the nature of the practice—that in any kind of practice a master or leader is needed. But at the same time, the attitude of Kapleau himself remains questionable; so long as he is attached to his own experience, there remains a question. As to the problem of interpretation of experience, I think that without experience there can be no interpretation. So when you interpret something, there must be some kind of experience within you. If somebody comments on your interpretation without looking into the inner side, then his comment is not valid. It is the same with D. T. Suzuki. People find fault with him, saying that when he interpreted Zen he overlooked the importance of experience, but it's not so. Without experience there can be no interpretation, and such things must be taken into account.

A.G.: So I am in good company, with Dr. Suzuki?

R.K.: Yes, that's right. About the so-called experience, in my view there seems to be one's own standpoint, which can never be understood or sympathized with by others. For example, the experience of having lost one's child could never be understood by others. There is no language with which to express the sorrow or grief of the experience of having lost one's own child. Such a thing I experienced in my dialogues with the late Dr. Suzuki. When I expressed my own view about the religious experience, Dr. Suzuki did not accept it, but he himself has expressed similar or identical things in his own way. If the same experience can be expressed by some others, it will not be described exactly like your experience. And in that sense experience is individual. Dogen expressed the necessity of discipline after Enlightenment. He said that you need further practice after attaining awareness. This means that so-called Enlightenment alone is not sufficient. You need eternal practice. In Japanese there are two terms used to express experience: *taiken* and *keiken*. I prefer the latter, *keiken*. Everybody has his own experience, perhaps religious experience, but the expression is different according to the individual. Of course, the ultimate religious standpoint for me is that of the Pure Land Faith, which is not an abstract one, but is a religious experience amid the joys and sorrows of this life. Apart from the daily experience, there is no religious life, so Satori is an occurrence of daily life, with its joys and sorrows.

A.G.: And by practice you mean the experience of everyday life, is that right?

R.K.: Yes. Let me express my own view of religion.

A.G.: That's what I want to hear.

R.K.: Ordinarily it is said that religion must be above all cultural phenomena and religion must lead, being transcendent over all cultural phenomena. According to that view, the sacred is beyond, or over and above, the true, the good, and the beautiful. According to that way of looking, religion is something equal to a judge or that which shows a norm or standard by which to judge all other things. But I am against such an idea, now current among intellectuals. Rather, I think that religion is something like a stream or undercurrent giving humidity or fertilizing the ground underlying all cultural phenomena. And, rather than judging, it aspires from beneath, so that everything may be better, much higher, much nobler. For art, for instance, religion seeks that it may be much better, much higher, much more beautiful. For ethics, religion hopes that ethics may be much more perfected, may become much more noble. So religion is not something that judges, but something that wishes, that prays, so that all cultural phenomena may be raised up.

A.G.: Within that view must there not be some ultimate viewpoint or ultimate reality, which is reached through Enlightenment, in order to *know* how to raise art or raise ethics, as the case might be? Mustn't there be some ultimate insight?

R.K.: It is difficult to name it, to point to it, or to express what it is, but this can be said, that the deepest, the lowest, is at once the highest. That is the source of religious awareness. At first sight it seems to be very paradoxical, but in religious consciousness it is not a contradiction, but a reality. The reason why the lowest can be at once the highest is difficult to say, but it is the ultimate reality of religious experience. And only from that awareness can the religious sense of blessedness—*arigatai*, in Japanese—be explained. Thankfulness, humility, gratitude—that awareness is the source of these religious sentiments. The relationship between the highest and lowest may be compared to the relationship between parents and child, or Amida and Dharmakara Bodhisattva, relationships in which the highest is well versed in the things of the lowest level. Very often in Jodo, Pure Land Buddhism, that relationship is expressed in terms of parent-child relationship. In order for parents to be parents they must become one with children. Unless parents completely identify themselves with children, they cannot be parents. In that sense the highest is expressed as Amida and the lowest is expressed as Hozo: the identity of the highest and lowest.

A.G.: That is very satisfying and concrete, very existential.

Visit of Dom Aelred Graham
to Yamada Mumon Roshi at Myoshin-ji Temple,
Kyoto, October 2, 1967.

Professor Masao Abe translated.

A.G.:   Professor Abe, you made some reference to my book *Zen Catholicism,* which was not in any way a kind of mixing together of Zen and Catholicism, but an enquiry as to whether the Zen insight could be applied to the structure of Catholicism with a view to bringing it more to light. So I would like to ask the Roshi if he can tell me his own view, or as much as he can say in words, of the central Zen experience. Satori—what it is, whether it is a thing of the mind or of the whole personality, and how it can be recognized. I'd like him to say as much as he could about that.

Y.R.:   Both body and mind must once die out. And only after that will the real new mind be resurrected.

A.G.:   That is a saying of Dogen's, isn't it? "The body and mind must fall away." I think I appreciate something of that. Could it be approached another way? How does a Roshi recognize when one of his students or disciples has become enlightened?

Y.R.:   In Zen there is a formal way of testing the disciple or monk to see whether or not he really has reached Enlightenment. That is koan testing. Strictly speaking, sometimes even when a disciple passes through a particular koan he may not be said to attain Enlightenment, so that is an important question.

A.G.: Would it be possible to attain Enlightenment without the use of the koan discipline? I understand there is one form of Zen that doesn't actually use the koan.

Y.R.: The koan was devised later in the history of Zen, in the Sung dynasty. Before then there was no such thing as a koan, and people came to Enlightenment through natural or spontaneous means. However, the koan was invented as a way to guide the disciple to Enlightenment.

A.G.: To change the subject slightly: would you think it possible to reach Enlightenment outside the Buddhist tradition—say, in the Christian tradition?

Y.R.: It is possible to attain Enlightenment outside the Buddhist tradition. For instance, poets and painters and artists in the West sometimes come to a point that is very close to Zen experience.

A.G.: Would that seem to link the Zen experience with the artistic, the aesthetic, the intellectual spheres of life rather than with the moral perhaps, or rather than with the total personality? The question arises in my mind: what of the Christian saints, some of them? You mention artists and painters and poets, and I'm sure there's a lot in that; but what about the Christian saints or the Sufi saints? Would they have Enlightenment?

Y.R.: From the Buddhist viewpoint, everyone has the Buddha nature—that is, the nature that enables him to awaken to his original face or to attain Enlightenment. So, whether Westerner or Easterner, the man of any religious tradition, from the Buddhist viewpoint, can attain Enlightenment. But this is a matter of the principle. In actuality, someone may attain Enlightenment rather easily, while someone else with difficulty. And if someone clings to some special way of thinking or way of life, he may find difficulty in attaining Enlightenment. So it is up to his life-attitude. In my own experience and observation, I find that while it is rather difficult for Germans to get Enlightenment, it is easier for the French.

A.G.: What about the English?

Y.R.: A middle way! A young Englishman who was doing Zazen at Daitoku-ji Temple came to see me. When I asked him "What are you doing in Zazen practice?" he said that he was doing Su soku kan. That is the practice of counting breaths. I asked him how well he was doing. He said, "I can count only five and cannot continue the practice any farther, because various concepts appear and I lose the way in counting." But I said, "Oh, next after five is just six, you know. How do you manage to lose count?"

A.G.:   Very good. We talked with a psychiatrist who has been living in Kyoto for a number of years. He said that Zen was strong, he thought, on the *prajna*, wisdom, aspect of Buddhism, but it wasn't strong, was deficient, in terms of *karuna*, compassion. What would be your comment on that?

Y.R.:   This is a very important comment. Dr. D. T. Suzuki also complained that the present form of Japanese Zen is lacking in *karuna*. However, I believe that it is not true Zen if it is lacking *karuna*, because the Zen experience is nothing but to become one with things or other people. So things or other persons are not things or other people, but one's own self. Compassion, therefore, is the essential matter for Zen. In the contemporary scene of Japanese Zen, even many Zen Masters are lacking more or less in the *karuna* aspect, in helping others. But I emphasize the importance and necessity of this aspect.

M.A.:   May I add something in this respect? As I said, Yamada Roshi is very active in helping others in various ways: delivering sermons, taking care of students, encouraging peace movements, helping sick people. In particular he is helping lepers in the leper colony on an island in the Inland Sea.

A.G.:   That recalls the position of Saint Thomas Aquinas. He says that the contemplative life is better than the active life in itself. But the best of all lives is when activity flows from a superabundance of contemplation. I think that the great Zen tradition may be misrepresented in certain parts of the United States. A book has come out by Philip Kapleau, which is sometimes spoken of as having replaced any earlier book on Zen. It seems to me the whole stress of that book is on personal self-perfection. He says the individual should be able to face death with "dignity and composure," to face the atomic bomb, for instance. But he doesn't seem to show any concern for trying to prevent the atomic bomb from falling.

Y.R.: Dr. Suzuki disagreed with Philip Kapleau.

A.G.: One hears that great violence seems to be used in the Zendo to try to promote or force, bring along quickly, the Kensho experience, and that that is particularly the case in the Yasutani-Roshi tradition or way of handling things.

M.A.: You think that that violence is particular to Yasutani's way?

A.G.: It particularly comes out in Philip Kapleau's book. He seems to have almost an obsession with the use of the *keisaku* in the Zendo. I would like to understand the practice better than I do. I don't understand it well, and I think it lends itself to abuse, you see, almost sadism. Could you say something to enlighten a Westerner like myself about that?

Y.R.: The *keisaku* is used partly for awakening the sitter who is falling asleep. Properly speaking, it should be administered on the request of the person who is sitting. However, if the monk does not realize that he is sleeping, then the one who is watching may give him a blow. The present usage of the *keisaku* in the United States by Japanese monks seems to me to be a demonstration of the peculiarity of Zen for the purpose of showing what Zen is like. It is something like a gesture. But it must be used more carefully and in a more proper way.

A.G.: Is Zen making much appeal nowadays to the young people of Japan? Are many young men coming to be students at Zen temples and monasteries?

Y.R.: The interest in Zen is greatly increasing among the younger generation.

A.G.: I understand that might be something of a feedback from the United States. I was told that so many American young people are interested in Zen that the Japanese are realizing that perhaps there could be something in it.

Y.R.: I have often said that the present form of Japanese Zen is not good; it's out. So it must be exported to the United States

M

and then imported again to Japan. Then there may be a revival in the Japanese form of Zen. Traditionally, it is said that Buddhism is always moving toward the east: from India to China, from China to Japan. So now Buddhism is moving from Japan to the United States, moving always eastward. So Zen should move to the United States and flourish there.

A.G.: It has also been said to us here in Kyoto that Zen goes along with any government or establishment power structure that exists, that it isn't really a liberating influence in society. It doesn't make people critical of wrong or undesirable forms of government; nor does it produce a mind critical toward society. I understand the hippies in San Francisco are not pleased with Zen now because they feel that the Zen people are not critical of government but go along with it as long as they can have their own private spiritual lives. The great religious thinkers, Jesus and Sakyamuni, were critical of the power structures around them. But it is said that Zen does not foster that. It doesn't make people alert to abuses in the government; it doesn't make them critical of the way money is spent, of the capitalist structure of a war such as the Vietnam war. Zen practitioners just say, "The government says we must be allies of the United States," or "We must go to war in Vietnam," and that's the end of it.

Y.R.: What you said about Zen being uncritical of the governmental authority is the case of the present form of Zen as well as of Japanese Buddhism in general. But I think that this is not the authentic way of Zen and Buddhism. We must get rid of such present forms. The proper attitude of Zen toward governmental institutions or policies is not to fight against them or to oppose them for the sake of opposition, but to embrace them and to guide them in the right direction. In the history of Japanese Zen some outstanding Zen Masters criticized the government of their time. Muso Kokushi, the founder of Tenryu-ji and Shokoku-ji, was the spiritual guide for the Shogun Ashikaga Takauji, but he often made very severe criticisms of the policy of the Shogunate. So by standing behind the politicians, the Zen Masters often gave spiritual guidance to their policy or behavior. Not

fighting against them but guiding them in the right direction is
the Zen way of dealing with political affairs.

A.G.:   I suppose it's never happened in history that the Zen insight
or tradition has had to make its way in a democratic society. The
case you mention is of somebody being a spiritual adviser to the
powers that be, and it is good to hear of that happening, of
somebody opposing the central power. But I suppose the problem now is to encourage people—young Japanese, for instance,
or students of Zen anywhere in the world, the kind of people
who can, with compassion and love, still criticize the powers that
be—to voice their criticisms in speech and in letters to the press,
or in the ordinary democratic procedures that are so familiar in
the West. Would you agree with that? Democracy is relatively
new in Japan, and perhaps the Zen tradition has still to find its
way there somehow. Could that be right?

Y.R.:   In the present democratic society it is necessary to appeal to
the masses, the ordinary people, emphasizing peace. The idea of
democracy and peace is not different from the idea of Zen itself.

M.A.:   As I said, Yamada Roshi, unlike other Zen Masters, is very
active in preaching and delivering sermons to people in various
places, and encouraging peace movements as well.

Y.R.:   When I say the masses I mean that cabinet ministers may
be included in the term. The Zen Master of today must appeal
to ordinary people, including the cabinet ministers, emphasizing
what is the right way for Japan. Zen has no idea of standing or
fighting against government for the purpose of opposition or re-
sistance, but of directing ordinary people, with the understanding that cabinet ministers are also included among them, in the
right way.

A.G.:   And presumably the right way is the way of the fully enlightened man, is that right?

Y.R.:   At this present moment I am especially emphasizing peace.
I disagree with Prime Minister Sato, who tells the people that
Japan now has become very prosperous, thanks to the alliance
with the United States. I do not think so. Sato's understanding
is something like this: our family becomes rich because we are

the second wife of a rich husband. I believe that we should be friendly with Red China as well as the United States. It should be a job for Japanese statesmen to act as intermediaries between China and the United States and to reconcile them to each other for the sake of world peace. That is my opinion, which I am always emphasizing in preaching to the people. So I have sometimes been condemned as "Red," or Communist, but I am not a Communist. I am presenting my belief. If my view is accepted by many people, the present governmental policy may be criticized by many.

A.G.: Perhaps the Prime Minister should come here and practice Zazen.

Y.R.: There is an alternative to the possibility of the Prime Minister coming here: I may be put in prison.

Conversation between the Reverend Shojun Bando
and Dom Aelred Graham at Ho-on-ji, Higashi Ueno,
Tokyo, October 14, 1967.

A.G.: Reverend Bando, it's a great pleasure and privilege for us to
be here as your guests at this temple. As you know, I'm here in
Japan not to deliver any message, but to learn something, particularly about the great Buddhist tradition in Japan. Very largely
with your help, we have seen a fair amount of the Buddhist
scene, particularly through interviews with a number of Zen
Roshis and other Zen practitioners. I would be grateful if you
could tell us first something of the specific emphasis of the tradition that you represent here in Tokyo, perhaps even with some
comments on its distinctiveness from Zen. Then perhaps we
could move on to the contemporary Buddhist scene in Japan.

S.B.: We are also very glad to receive you here. First I should like
to say something about what I think is the relationship between
the traditional Zen Buddhism and the Jodo-shin-shu, True Pure
Land, which we represent. I think I told you, at the Miyako
Hotel in Kyoto, that there is no fundamental difference between
Zen and Jodo-shin-shu. In Zen itself there are several schools
with different emphases on some aspect of the doctrine. These
days I realize the striking resemblance, similarity, between the
teachings by Dogen Zenji and Shinran Shonin. As I told you the

other day, the difference as I see it lies in the issue of oneness between the means and the end. In Zen there are three schools,
Soto, Rinzai, and Obaku, but Obaku is so small that it is negli-
gible here. Then Soto and Rinzai remain. In Rinzai Zen they use
koan as a means to attain Enlightenment, but in Soto Zen they
never use the koans. Soto Zen regards koans as a hindrance to
Enlightenment rather than a help.

A.G.: May I interrupt at this point? Didn't Dogen, the founder of
the Soto school, have koans, or didn't he have some experience
of them?

S.B.: He may have had experience in the practice of koans, but he
himself did not emphasize the importance of the koan. He negated its usefulness. Although he was a great scholar and a deep
philosopher, a profound thinker, he emphasized just sitting in
meditation, thinking of nothing in particular. For Dogen, a man
sitting in meditation is in the process of realizing the Buddha nature in himself. It is not that he will attain Enlightenment some-
time in the future after sitting in meditation, but that the Buddha nature is being realized in the process of meditation. So in
that respect, for Dogen, Zazen was at once the end and the
means. In Rinzai Zen, however, Zazen is only a means to an end,
and there can be a distance between these two. I think that is
the characteristic of the gradual awakening. Indeed, Rinzai Zen
emphasizes the importance of the abrupt awakening, and in
Rinzai the actual final awakening happens instantaneously, but
all the gradual training the trainee has undergone in the past becomes the content of the awakening. So the training is not useless, but has become the content of the awakening. In that sense,
means and end are unified, but no doubt there is still a fundamental gap between the means and the end.

A.G.: And which of those two schools, Rinzai or Soto, would be
nearer to your own tradition, Pure Land?

S.B.: Soto Zen is nearer to our standpoint than Rinzai, because
Shinran inherited the teaching of the Nembutsu from Honen,
his master, and Shinran himself declared . . .

A.G.: Shinran was the founder . . . ?

s.b.: The founder of Jodo-shin-shu. And Honen was the founder of Jodo Shu, Pure Land. Shinran was the foremost disciple of Honen. In later years Shinran often declared that he had nothing to teach; his mission in this world was just to convey what he had heard from his master, Honen, to his friends, and he had nothing new to teach others. He said that Jodo-shin-shu was started by Honen. So the teaching of Nembutsu was common to both Honen and Shinran, but in our eyes there is a fundamental difference between the thought of these two people. In Honen's teaching of Nembutsu there was a gap between the means and the end. For Honen, Nembutsu was a means to an end, which was Enlightenment. "If you recite the Nembutsu you will be enlightened": that was Honen's teaching. But Shinran's teaching differed on this point. Your recitation of the Nembutsu is nothing but proof of the realization of the Buddha's will in you. So Buddha's vow is moving in you.

a.g.: And what is the Buddha's vow? Is it one vow or many?

s.b.: Buddha's vow is usually expressed in forty-eight vows, but the fundamental spirit is one. That spirit is expressed: "Unless you attain Buddhahood, I will not attain Buddhahood. If there is anyone in illusion or suffering, then I cannot become enlightened in the true sense of the term."

a.g.: Unless everybody else does?

s.b.: Unless everybody else attains Enlightenment, I cannot truly attain Enlightenment, so my destiny and everybody's destiny are one. That is Amida's vow. Amida's vow is the fundamental vow, the basic vow of every one of us. We have many wishes, desires, wills; they are particular wishes and wills. But what is it that we really wish to do? What is our fundamental will? It was pointed out by the Buddha, the Enlightened One, that our fundamental will is expressed in this vow. It was pointed out by the Buddha and expressed in terms of forty-eight vows.

a.g.: What is the literal translation of Nembutsu in English?

s.b.: There is no fixed term for it. No English is suitable, because for the term *"nen"* there are many meanings: to think of the Buddha, to remember the Buddha's vow, to recite the name of the Buddha—all these meanings are contained in the term "Nembutsu." So it can vary according to the occasion.

A.G.: And is it part of the doctrine that saying Nembutsu once brings Enlightenment?

S.B.: Yes. To say Nembutsu once in sincerity is enough. The merit of reciting Nembutsu once and the merit of reciting the Nembutsu many times are not different, it is stated in the sutra. According to the human mind, the more the better, but in the eyes of the Buddha the merit is equal in both cases.

A.G.: And which is the sutra on which this is based?

S.B.: Dai Muryoju-kyo, the Larger Sukhavati Vyuha Sutra. In the Sanskrit original the number "ten times" appears. It means recitation of Nembutsu ten times, but it is the symbol of plural recitation, so it covers any number. This is our understanding.

A.G.: Well now, let us pass to the contemporary Buddhist scene in Japan. Would you say that Buddhism in general has considerable vitality now, today?

S.B.: Yes. My view of present-day Buddhism is that . . . First of all I should say that true Buddhism cannot be grasped in terms of time. So the term "present-day Buddhism" itself is contradictory. Also, I think I have a question all the time, which is: Who is to judge whether Buddhism is flourishing or not? If it is judged by the illusory mind, then the judgment will not be trustworthy. The one who is qualified to judge must have some special qualification; he must have the spiritual eye. The Reverend Kaneko once said that there are many who say that Buddhism is stagnant at present, is not flourishing at present, but isn't it that Buddhism is not flourishing in those people only?

A.G.: In other words, only the enlightened man can judge whether Buddhism is flourishing or not. That's the position?

S.B.: Also, what will be the standard by which to judge the prosperity or decline of Buddhism? I don't think you can judge the flourishing of Buddhism by the number of people gathering. Many people can gather at a temple whose teachings are very superstitious or doubtful. So the standard must be somewhere else. Once, the Eighth Patriarch of the Jodo-shin-shu, Rennyo, said that the fact that many people gather at a temple is not the mark of the flourishing of Buddhism. If even one person attains Enlightenment, this is the mark of the flourishing of Buddhism. Rennyo's admonition that we should be careful about external phenomena is famous. He always rejected reliance upon external phenomena; his standard was only in the unseen.

A.G.: There are parallels to that in the sayings of Jesus: "The Kingdom of God is within you" and "Where two or three are gathered together, there am I in the midst of you." That's the same sort of thing, isn't it?

S.B.: Yes. Also, the Buddha said, "One who sees the truth of dependent origination sees me, and one who sees me sees the Dharma." In that case "Dharma" meant the law of dependent origination.

A.G.: Is it possible to elucidate a little that very complex theme of dependent origination?

S.B.: I doubt if I have the ability, if I'm competent enough to do that.

A.G.: Well, that's a very good start.

S.B.: I will try my best. The Russian Buddhist scholar Stcherbatsky translated the term "Pratitya Samutpada" as "relativity." But as in most other cases, such a translation is partial only. Pratitya Samutpada, or in other words, "dependent origination," has an aspect of relativity, but that is not all. It is not a state of things, but is a living reality, a very dynamic reality, and if you translate the term as "relativity," you have the impression that reality is very static. Dr. Ui, a famous Buddhist scholar and the foremost authority on Buddhism in recent times, said that the true meaning of Pratitya Samutpada is not "arising"—it does not point to the act of arising, but to the dynamic fact of reality as such.

A.G.: Would it be "things are mutually causing one another"—something like that?

S.B.: Yes, exactly.

A.G.: That doctrine would seem to eliminate a creator distinct from the world, would it not?

S.B.: Yes, it would exclude the notion. According to the Buddhist way of thinking, the idea of creator is only one supposition. Instead of the world arising by innumerable or an inconceivable number of conditions, instead of pointing to the totality of those conditions, and to simplify the expression of creation, the term "God" was adopted. It is very much in the nature of supposition. That is our view.

A.G.: And you would regard it as an oversimplification, would you?

S.B.: Yes, in a way. We think it is only one choice from many other interpretations.

A.G.: I'd love to hear comments from your point of view, and according to your knowledge, on these new religions in Japan. You must have had some contact with them.

S.B.: There are many kinds of new religions. I know some very excellent people who are believers in some new faiths like Kodo Kyodan and Rissho Kosei-Kai. If I judge in my own way the quality of these faiths, I can affirm their merit, but when I see some of the followers who go to the extreme, I cannot approve. If I see the central figures, the leading people, who are very excellent people, I think I can perceive some truth in them. In the case of Soka Gakkai, I am not well acquainted with their teaching and I must depend on what I hear from people, so I'm not in a position to evaluate it properly.

A.G.: Is Soka Gakkai making a great impact on the life of Japan, do you think?

S.B.: Yes, but now it seems that they have entered into the second stage. The first stage was rapid expansion. It made a great impact upon people in general. But now they seem to be concentrating on various tasks of co-ordinating their system, and the impact upon people seems to be less.

A.G.: Soka Gakkai doesn't have very much appeal to scholars, intellectuals, thoughtful people, does it?

S.B.: On some intellectuals it made a great impact, but not on the majority.

A.G.: It is in the Buddhist tradition, isn't it?

S.B.: They claim it to be. But if they admit the use of violence to convert people, I don't think it is Buddhistic.

A.G.:   What is to be said of Nichiren? Isn't he the forefather?

S.B.:   His violent proselytizing activities arise largely from his own character.

A.G.:   He appealed to one of the great sutras, didn't he? Was it the Lotus Sutra?

S.B.:   Yes. He claimed to be the embodiment of the spirit of the Lotus Sutra.

A.G.:   And what is to be said about the Lotus Sutra? Is it early or late? Is it in the central Buddhist tradition?

S.B.:   It is said that that sutra belongs to the later time in the Buddha's life. In that sutra it is stated, "For the past forty years I have preached various kinds of teaching, but they are Upaya."

A.G.:   Which means "devices"?

S.B.:   Yes, provisional means employed by the Buddha in order to lead unenlightened people. Then he said, "But what I'm going to say is the final truth." The Buddha himself says so in the Saddharma Pundarika Sutra. So, since long ago, this sutra has been regarded as the highest of all Mahayana sutras. But this depends on interpretation. All other schools based on other sutras do not approve of the Tendai-shu or Nichiren-Shu standpoint. Tendai-shu is also based on the Lotus Sutra.

A.G.:   What are the other new religions? Most of them achieved vitality since the war, isn't that right?

S.B.:   Yes, since the war.

A.G.:   This was a response to the depressed situation of Japan then. But there's a good deal of Buddhism in most of them, isn't there? Much more of Buddhism than Christianity, is that right?

S.B.:   Yes, much more Buddhism than Christianity. I think the order may be Buddhist, Shinto, and Christian.

A.G.:   And do they all, or most of them, reverence the historical figure of Sakyamuni?

S.B.:   Yes. Without it a school can't be called Buddhism. Sakyamuni must have a position.

A.G.:   So that it would be true even today that the central religious tradition of Japan is Mahayana Buddhism?

S.B.:   Yes, Mahayana.

A.G.:   Reverend Bando, you've been to the United States, and

Continental Europe and England, and you've held dialogues
with Christians. Do you think that Buddhism has anything to
learn from Christianity, or Christianity from Buddhism?

s.b.:   I think I can say what Buddhism should learn from Christianity but not vice versa.

a.g.:   Very good! That's worth hearing.

s.b.:   I think the basis of Buddhist teaching is *karuna*, compassion,
but to what extent that spirit is lived by people, by alleged Buddhists, is questionable. *Karuna* must be realized in concrete ways,
in social institutions, social-welfare activities, or acts of charity. In
that respect Buddhism is far behind Christianity. The Buddhist
teaching of compassion must be realized in social aspects, social
practice, and in that respect Buddhism should learn more from
Christianity. Otherwise the ideal will become just an illusory
dream. The ideal must be substantiated by actual practice.

a.g.:   So far as one can observe and presume to judge, which seem
the more compassionate or the more to realize the point that
you're now making, individual Christians or individual Buddhists? I understand your point that Buddhist compassion needs
to be more organized and to express itself through institutions in
the way that happens with Christians. What I'm now asking is if
in the ordinary intercourse of person with person you have observed or come to any tentative conclusions about whether
Christians are more friendly and outgoing and compassionate in
their relations with one another?

s.b.:   It varies according to country, according to which class of
people you associate with. It varies. You can't generalize.

a.g.:   I'm sure that's so. About what Christians can learn from
Buddhists, my own feeling is, as I've tried to express in a book of
mine, that Christians need to attach less importance to formularies and to doctrinal statements. I think Christianity is much
more of an ideology than Buddhism is. Would that be your impression?

s.b.:   Yes.

a.g.:   That it's much more in the world of ideas, rather hard, set
ideas, Platonic ideas, you might say; and that it lacks the con-

creteness and the existential quality, perhaps, of Buddhism.

S.B.: But it could be said to have the Indian metaphysical tendency.

A.G.: Do you think the Hindu approach is similar to the Catholic Scholastic approach? I hope to discover something about that. Nagarjuna, for example.

H.T.: You would think that the Indian Buddhist thinkers are analogous in the sense of working out ideas?

S.B.: Not in the same sense. For example, the writers of the Nirvana Sutra and the writers of the Avatamsaka Sutra sometimes become very abstract.

A.G.: Zen here in Japan is against all that sort of thing, isn't it? It almost brushes aside the sutras, although it's based on one or two of them, isn't it?

S.B.: Yes. When Zen goes to the extreme, some Zen Roshis despise the scholars. But scholarship should not be totally neglected, I believe. If they dismiss scholarship from the beginning, they will fall into a sort of dogmatism.

H.T.: I would like to ask if the new religions, such as Soka Gakkai, teach a world view including Pratitya Samutpada? Although you say they are Buddhist in the sense that they reverence the historical Gautama, do they teach the original content of the Dharma?

S.B.: I am not quite sure. According to some religious papers, it is said that Soka Gakkai neglects the significance of the historical Gautama Buddha, and even totally dismisses it, emphasizing the importance of the eternal nature of the Buddha.

H.T.: Not his view of life?

S.B.: Of course they have high regard for Gautama's teaching, but they emphasize the importance of the transcendent nature of the Buddha so much that they sometimes say they can dispense with the historical Buddha. It is contradictory: without the historical Buddha we cannot understand the teachings of the Buddha. Thanks to the efforts of the historical Buddha, we are enabled to know the eternal Dharma. So it is not right for them to dismiss the historical Buddha altogether.

A.G.: Another aspect of Buddhism from which I think Christians

can learn a good deal is the stress on Enlightenment and the
purified mind. Christianity since the Reformation has stressed
the will, effort, the devotional life, the observance of ecclesiastical precepts and that sort of thing, but it hasn't much developed
the human understanding in depth. That is a breakaway from
the medieval Christian, Catholic, tradition, where people like
Thomas Aquinas and Eckhart were absolutely committed to the
supremacy of the intelligence and of the enlightened mind. So
you get Hindu-Buddhist scholars like Coomaraswamy emphasizing that medieval Catholic thinkers talked the same language,
were on the same wave length as the Great Hindu and Buddhist
thinkers. I think something of that kind has to be recaptured in
the Christian church, where most of the discussion nowadays
seems to be in terms of intramural dialogues about the nature of
ecclesiastical authority and church ritual, the place of popes and
bishops and the laity. All of this has some relative importance,
but it leaves out the preoccupations of the great medieval Catholic thinkers with God and with man and with nature. They were
very little interested in the institutional church or popes and
bishops. So I think that perhaps from Buddhism, the Buddhist
insight, Christians could learn quite a lot today.

S.B.: However, hearing you talk, and reflecting on the Buddhist
circle itself, I find that in the present day most of the Buddhists
are getting more and more occupied with immediate things,
things just in front of them. They tend less and less to think of
eternity or human nature or the final destiny of man, and so
forth. They tend less and less to think of fundamental things,
and they are inclined to worry about external things—institutions, means of propagation, and the system of the order. These
things are important in themselves, but I think they should get
much more interested in fundamental things.

A.G.: Before concluding this most valuable discussion, there are
two further points that I'd like to raise with you, Reverend
Bando. In our encounters with Zen Roshis and authorities on
Zen in Kyoto and elsewhere, there has been unanimity on one

matter: that the Roshi knows when the disciple or student has reached Enlightenment and that he is in a position to certify that. From my Western background that is very difficult for me to understand. I wonder if from your tradition of Buddhism you could comment on that.

S.B.: I think Enlightenment can be judged only by the Buddhas, and it is one of the wonders for us Pure Land Buddhists to see some Zen monks highly confident of their qualification to judge the disciple's Enlightenment. I think it can be done, to some extent, even by the beginners in faith. Some intuitive understanding may be had by ordinary believers, but how far that judgment is accurate is open to question, I think. Insofar as even Zen Roshis are human beings, I don't think their judgment can be one hundred per cent correct.

A.G.: The other question arises from another comment made to us during these discussions. The view has been offered that Christianity is really better adjusted to the Japanese temperament than Buddhism is, and that it is just historical accident that Buddhism has dominated the scene—historical accident in the sense that Buddhism got here first and won the minds of the Japanese people. Would you care to comment on that?

S.B.: It depends upon the definition of the word "adjusted." If it means intellectual understanding, then such a statement may be justified to some extent. But I don't think so. Buddhism is far better appreciated and digested and made the flesh and blood of the Japanese people.

A.G.: Yes, I agree that that seems to be so. But from your study of Christianity, would you say that this necessarily is so? Do you think that there are some elements in Christianity that are uncongenial to the Japanese temperament?

S.B.: Yes. What comes to my mind first is that the Japanese people generally do not like to have in their way of thinking the sharp distinction between good and evil, right and wrong, friend and enemy. I think the Christian way of thinking tends to raise such distinctions. The Japanese seem to leave things as they are;

however vague a thing may seem, the Japanese do not like to make sharp distinctions between the opposites.

A.G.: That corresponds to what I've heard elsewhere in this visit to Japan, that the phrase "religious syncretism" is rather a good idea.

S.B.: Ah, do you think so?

A.G.: I ask you!

S.B.: The other day when I was talking with my father, this point happened to be raised: that Shintoism and Buddhism are coexistent in Japan, in Japanese families. Both Shinto and Buddhist deities are enshrined in one family. Looking at this phenomenon, foreigners may interpret it as being religious syncretism, but we Japanese don't think so. It is simply a matter taken for granted. If Shintoism is regarded as a religion in the sense that Christianity is, then it may be said to be a phenomenon of religious syncretism. But in our consciousness there is no such idea of religion about Shintoism. Shinto gods, as we think about them, are those people who contributed a great deal to the community in which they were born or who have made a particular contribution to certain interests of the neighborhood, nation, village, or town. During the wartime, when soldiers died at the front, they were all called gods, *kamis* in Japanese. So a Japanese *kami* is not the Christian God. In that respect it can be said that Shintoism is not a religion in the sense that Christianity is. So, in Shintoism not one almighty god is worshiped, but many, innumerable *kamis* are worshiped—we call them "innumerable *kamis*." It may correspond to the Buddhist worship of Buddhas and Bodhisattvas and other deities; so they are not contradictory to each other. In the minds of the Japanese there is no sense of contradiction at all.

A.G.: It is a question of synthesis rather than syncretism?

S.B.: Yes. I think so. Shintoism and Buddhism have come down to the present day on friendly terms. Neither one attempted to extinguish the other.

A.G.: I thought at the beginning of the Meiji era there was some attack by the Shintoists on the Buddhists.

s.b.: Yes. Some fanatic people spread the idea, and there were some attacks in many parts of Japan, but somehow or other Buddhism survived.

N

Conversation between the Reverend Shojun Bando,
Dom Gabriel Furuta, and Dom Aelred Graham
at International House, Tokyo, October 16, 1967.

A.G.: I have the happy opportunity of having as guests two
friends, the Reverend Shojun Bando, a dedicated Buddhist of
the Pure Land sect and Dr. Gabriel Furuta, a fellow Benedictine
but also a Japanese who understands the Japanese scene; and I'm
wondering if we can perhaps exchange a few ideas about my experiences in what has been a kind of dialogue between Christianity
and Buddhism. My understanding is that the devotion to Amida
Buddha as expressed by the Pure Land sect is fairly close in some
ways to Christianity, and that there is something distinctive in
that aspect of the Buddhist tradition from, let us say, Zen, which
is a little more remote perhaps, or more austere. I would be very
glad to have Reverend Bando's views on the Pure Land tradition, with some reference to Christianity, which he has studied
and which he has observed in the West. Then, perhaps, Dr. Furuta would make some comment on what Reverend Bando
might have to say.

S.B.: Just a little time ago the Reverend Furuta asked me if I
think Buddhism is a religion.

A.G.: That's a very pertinent question.

S.B.: And to this question I should say that in the ordinary sense of the word "religion" I think Buddhism or Jodo-shin-shu is a religion. But strictly speaking, if the word "religion" is taken to mean "union," union of two things into one, such as God and man, then I don't think Buddhism or Jodo-shin-shu is a religion. According to the Buddhist conception, fundamentally religion is not two things becoming one, but is just the realization that the two we have regarded as being different have been from the beginning one. So, realization of two things as originally or fundamentally being one is the basic conception of *shukyo*, or religion.

A.G.: And what are the two things in this case?

S.B.: Amida and "I." Amida, which is usually regarded as opposed to human beings.

G.F.: Well, Reverend Bando, do you think somehow or other we can trace these two poles? Trace in this sense, that perhaps there was and has been, and there is even now, some kind of psychological experience when man realizes that he is not a unity—there is some kind of division inside himself.

S.B.: Yes, it is true. And actually the starting point of Buddhism is the realization of this differentiation. When we suffer, the suffering is attributed to our sense of differentiation. Why we suffer is because we differentiate things, and that is the starting point of Buddhism.

A.G.: Would it be true to say that Amida is, in modern psychological language, a projection of the individual?

S.B.: Probably not.

A.G.: Is he, to some extent, an object of worship, a source of help to appeal to? Whereas, according to the Christian way of thinking, Jesus of Nazareth, our Lord, as we call him, is a historical figure. What would be the Buddhist comment on the sense Christians have that Jesus of Nazareth is, at least to begin with, distinct from us Christians?

S.B.: I think Amida should be contrasted not with Jesus but with God, and Jesus with Gautama. This reminds me of the Buddhist conception of Tri-kaya, the three bodies of the Buddha. According to that idea, God may be compared to Dharma-kaya, truth itself, and Jesus may be compared to Nirmana-kaya or the incarnation of truth.

H.T.:   Would there be anything to be said about the Sambhoga-kaya in that comparison?

S.B.:   Yes. These days I have been inquiring into the exact meaning of the three bodies. I found out that Dharma-kaya is the truth itself and Nirmana-kaya is human form. So what is Sambhoga-kaya? The last question has been a problem of mine for a long time. I asked the Reverend Kaneko the other day, "What is the exact meaning of Sambhoga-kaya?" According to the old interpretation of these three terms, it is said that Dharma-kaya has no beginning and no end, Sambhoga-kaya has a beginning but no end, and Nirmana-kaya has a beginning and an end. Very often Dharma-kaya is said to be truth itself, beginningless, endless, eternal, and Sambhoga-kaya is said to be something like Amida. Amida, according to the Buddhist scripture, was once a king. After long practice, he attained Buddhahood. So he has a beginning as a human being and no end, and that's why he is still teaching us, eternally. He is existing as the teaching, therefore he has no end. Nirmana-kaya may be compared to Sakyamuni Buddha, the historical figure, who led exactly the same life as ours. He has a beginning and an end. But I was not satisfied with this kind of explanation. I asked the Reverend Kaneko, and I found out that these three bodies are one in the sense that when we revere somebody as the incarnation or messenger of the Buddha, then he was born as a human being; in that sense he has a beginning. But after he attained Buddhahood, he passed away like our ancestors. So, they were born as human beings—in that sense they had a beginning; and they died as human beings—in that sense they had an end. But at present they are still living, since their teaching is still teaching us. So Nirmana-kaya and Sambhoga-kaya are not two different things. Sakyamuni Buddha was Nirmana-kaya when he lived in India; all people looked upon him as a human being exactly like themselves. But when we, two thousand five hundred years later, look back on him, he is not a mere human being, but something more. So when we look back on Sakyamuni Buddha, he is

Sambhoga-kaya. The same person has three aspects. So although the three bodies are differentiated, they are one. That's my conclusion.

A.C.: That's a most valuable exposition of the three bodies of the Buddha, Reverend Bando. Would you care to comment or say something, Dr. Furuta?

G.F.: I would rather ask a few questions. The point is this: you mentioned that perhaps the Christ in Christianity can be compared to Nirmana-kaya in a way, because he has beginning and end.

S.B.: It points only to his human aspect.

G.F.: Humanness, yes, but according to the later . . .

S.B.: But apparently he was more than that.

G.F.: Yes, more that that. You know, living in Japan and thinking as a Japanese, and thinking about Christianity and the difficulties it is confronting now in Japan, I have always felt, and I still feel, that the difficulty is the lack of a sense of historicity on the part of the Japanese. I think the very keen historical sense in the West was started with Christ, if I'm not mistaken. Among Greeks, still, the meaning of history was a mere circular conception, but with Christ it became linear.

S.B.: The Greek way of thinking is similar to the Indian way.

G.F.: But with Christianity it is completely different. According to your exposition of the doctrine of the three bodies of the Buddha, it seems to me that the essential emphasis that Christianity puts upon Christ in terms of the historical person is still lacking. And this is not anything that you can just put aside, since it is so essential to Christianity. So, taking into account this point of historicity, do you think there is any possibility at all of Christianity being Japanized or orientalized?

H.T.: What would you consider the uniqueness of the historicity of Christ that the Nirmana-kaya aspect of the Tri-kaya doctrine can't include? Where does historicity escape that elucidation?

G.F.: You mean in Christianity itself?

H.T.: Yes. Where does the historicity of Christ break the bounds of the Tri-kaya doctrine?

G.F.: I think, for one thing, in Christianity Christ is the center, and his historical personality as such is something we tend to be absorbed into. And since Christ as a historical personality is still divine, our historicity is not an obstacle to our being absorbed into the historical person of Christ. But in Buddhistic teaching, it seems to me, the object is not so much being absorbed into a historical person as attaining some kind of a cognitive understanding of the teaching, which is quite different from the essential unity that we preach as being attained between Christians and Christ through grace. If this is not too bad an exposition of the Christian position, then there is a tremendous gap here. This is the kind of point that has always troubled me in considering dialogue—and not only such a high-flown discussion. Just preaching to common Japanese Christians, we have difficulty getting response.

S.B.: Yes. My feeling is that the general Japanese people received the teaching of Jesus as something particular—too particular. And the general attitude of oriental people toward particular things is that they assimilate particular things in terms of generality. To mention a concrete example: once the Abbot of Senso-ji Temple made a statement suggesting that Jesus of Nazareth is a Bodhisattva, according to the Buddhist conception. He *is* a Bodhisattva, but of course this is a Buddhist way of thinking, and Christians may not accept that kind of view. But I think such a statement may reveal something of the way that the average person who has a background of Buddhism thinks. It also reminds me of the Indians' general attitude toward Buddhism. In India they say that Buddha is the twenty-first incarnation of Vishnu (in another tradition the ninth), and that Buddhism belongs to Hinduism, and Hinduism and Buddhism are not two different things. This may point to something; it may account for the fact that Buddhism lost ground, lost its *raison d'être*, in India. It does not show that Buddhism completely perished in India, but according to the Indian way of thinking it is alive only in the context of Hinduism.

A.G.: Is the ultimate religion going to be in terms of Christianity or in terms of Buddhism? I entirely agree with Father Gabriel about the historical import of Jesus of Nazareth. To me it seems a very strong point that Jesus was actually a historical figure, who lived at a certain time and place, whereas Amida is conceived to be beyond history, comparable to the way the God of Christianity transcends space and time. On the other hand, I feel that Christians still have a good deal of thinking to do about what historicity amounts to and what exactly it means. I suppose even within the New Testament itself difficulties might arise between, let us say, Saint Mark's presentation and that of Saint John or Saint Paul. The three synoptic Evangelists were to some extent interested in the historical sequence of events, whereas Paul, who has colored the whole Christian scene, didn't seem to be terribly interested in the historical narrative—what exactly Jesus did from the time he was born till the time he died. He was interested simply in the death and resurrection of Christ. Do you think we have anything more to elucidate in those areas?

s.b.: Who made Christianity a universal religion?—bringing it out of the boundary of folk religion—and how did they do it? I think there may be a secret, some hint, some suggestion, embodied in that point that may be valid for the case of Christianity in Japan, which is now confronted with the problem of indigenization. What was the motive for Christianity to be made a universal religion, breaking the boundaries of folk religion? I think the overemphasis on particularity or the historicity of Jesus may be a stumbling block.

a.g.: What is meant by folk religion?

s.b.: A religion only for a certain race.

a.g.: For the Jewish people?

s.b.: Yes, the Jewish people. But later it was embraced by the Roman Empire and then gradually secured a ground in the whole of Europe. And finally it became a world religion. So I think the solution to the present problem, the problem of Christianity being indigenized, being absorbed by the Japanese climate, is not different from that motive. I think the problems are not two different things. I think it was Toynbee who insisted on that point: in order for Christianity to be a universal religion it must drop its insistence on the particularity.

a.g.: I think Toynbee would deny the uniqueness of Christianity and the uniqueness of the incarnation of the Divine in Jesus. I think he would say that Sakyamuni Buddha is just as much a revelation or embodiment of the Divine as Jesus of Nazareth.

s.b.: So in that respect, when Buddhism was introduced into Japan and Japanized in that process, I think there was a process of living through death. Buddhism renounced from the beginning its insistence upon uniqueness and, in that respect, killed itself from the beginning. So although there were some struggles between Shintoism and Buddhism at the beginning of this history, finally Buddhism survived. It was dead from the beginning, but finally it survived. So I think there is only one way for Christianity to survive or to develop in Japan, and that is to die.

a.g.: That's a very startling thought, Father.

g.f.: Yes, it is.

a.g.: Does anything immediately occur to you about it?

g.f.: I think that is exactly the kind of death throe we're going through at the present time. In our daily experiences we confront a sort of incomprehensibility on the part of the people to whom we talk about God or Christianity. Even when they accept, we know that they do not understand what we are speaking about. Christianity is coming to the point, historically speaking, when the preachers themselves do not know what to preach.

a.g.: Do you think a meeting ground could be, as was suggested in a group at the Sacred Heart College last night, in the area of the individual spiritual life and meditation? That if we Christians, we Catholics, learned more from Buddhists about the actual business of sitting in meditation quietly and stripping the mind of prejudices and desires we might get nearer to the heart of the matter? I remember meeting a Zen Master in Kyoto a week or so ago, and he said that as long as we are silent we agree, but as soon as we start to talk, we differ. So, perhaps, is there something to be said for being silent, do you think?

g.f.: Yes. In the silent depths perhaps we understand each other and we understand, perhaps, what we call "God." That's the reason why I asked at the beginning whether you consider Jodoshin-shu a religion. Because what we mean by religion is central to the question, in a way. There our problems converge. We are facing and we are moved by the same reality. But it is not so much how to understand, perhaps, as how to express what we understand.

s.b.: Yes. The interpretation.

g.f.: The interpretations are quite different.

s.b.: Only, in interpretation there is difference. But the same reality confronts us irrespective of the faith we profess.

g.f.: Because, like Shinran's teaching, if I'm not mistaken, the fact of a man's being led to recite the Nembutsu is the indication of his being saved. In Christianity, too, Saint Paul said that when a man does not believe, it is a sign that he is not saved. The fact of being led to someone is the indication that we are already in him.

s.b.: I understand that the implication of *Namu Amida Butsu* is almost equal to "Thy will be done," and when we say "*Namu Amida Butsu*," we say it in the state of mind of "Thy will be done," replacing our egos with the will of Amida. So I think that in that respect words differ but mind is one from the beginning.

g.f.: My difficulty still lies in assessing the meaning of historicity or the importance that historicity actually has to Christianity. It seems to me that historicity not only has had, but still has, some kind of central position in the way of Christian thinking, believing, and even feeling. It's not simply Western; it seems Christian.

a.g.: I think there's agreement now in what has been said by the Reverend Bando and Dr. Furuta that can be summed up in Pascal's phrase, or the alleged revelation of Jesus to Pascal: "Thou wouldst not seek me if thou hadst not already found me." About the question raised by Harold, I think the church still has to give a good deal more attention than is usually done to modern New Testament research on the personality of Jesus—what his message was and what he stood for. It seems now that there's agreement among scholars, at least German scholars, that the whole New Testament narrative really hinges around belief in Jesus as the Risen Lord, and so the Messiah, and that everything in the

Gospels and the Pauline Epistles is predicated on that belief that Jesus was the Messiah and the Risen Lord in heaven. That raises Jesus beyond the historical order in some way, and perhaps gives greater validity, although it's not directly intended by the scholars, to the ordinary Catholic proclamation that Jesus is the Incarnate Lord reigning in heaven, and so to some extent is not merely a historical but also an ideal figure. On that level of thought there may be closer links with the points that the Reverend Bando has been making, that the great realities of religion are praeter-historical, beyond history, that the person who is concerned with his own salvation or with his own Enlightenment is not looking back—the Buddhist is not looking back to Sakyamuni, and Christians are not really looking back to Christ, nor are they looking forward. They're living in the spirit of Christ and trusting God right now in the present moment. As the masters of the spiritual life, Father Caussade for instance, say, "Do what you're doing now, suffer what you're suffering now," that's the way to the ultimate Enlightenment, the ultimate holiness. Perhaps we have something more to learn about living in the present moment; and perhaps that's the meeting point between the Buddhist and the Christian traditions. Do you think there's anything in that?

s.b.: Buddhism, inheriting the assets of Indian spirituality, is highly inclined to be abstract and metaphysical, and in that respect I think Buddhism should learn more from Christianity—the concreteness. I don't think that the emphasis on the historicity of Jesus is a bad thing; I think it is very important so that we may not . . . go up.

a.g.: Be up in the clouds.

s.b.: Up into the clouds. If we become too abstract, then religiousness itself is lost, because religion is something which should be rooted in reality at the present moment. In that respect, I think Buddhism should learn more concreteness from Christianity, so that it may not forget the everyday mind.

a.g.: "The everyday mind, that is the way." And the Our Father is rather linked, isn't it, with the everyday mind?

G.F.: Yes. Just as concrete as bread.

A.G.: That's right. "Give us this day our daily bread." Exactly. Well, perhaps, with the Our Father, that's a good way of concluding this little discussion.

Some Terms and Names
That May Call for Explanation

Abhidharma: A development of Buddhist doctrine, probably formulated within two centuries of the Buddha's death; later codified, in the 5th century A.D., by Vasubandhu (*q.v.*).

Ahimsa: Non-injury, harming no living thing; taught and exemplified notably in modern times by Mahatma Gandhi, in terms of non-violent civil disobedience.

Amida Buddha: From the Sanskrit *Amitabha*, the glorified Buddha, the savior of the faithful; focus of worship of Pure Land (*q.v.*) Buddhists.

Amitabha: See above.

Anatta theory: Buddhist doctrine which holds that the apparent individual self is unreal.

Asanga: Brother of Vasubandhu. In the 5th century A.D. they systematized the Yogacara (*q.v.*) school of Buddhism.

Ashvaghosa: Supposedly the author of a comprehensive summary of Mahayana Buddhism, *The Awakening of Faith*, which recent scholarship dates as of the 6th century A.D.

Asoka: Celebrated Indian emperor converted to Buddhism in the 3rd century B.C. who proved a most effective patron of the Buddhist faith and sent missionaries to Ceylon and Southeast Asia.

Atman: Hindu term meaning the sub-stratum of consciousness, the self, apparently distinguishable from, but in reality identical with, the supreme being, Brahman.

Avalokitesvara: "He who looks down with compassion," *i.e.*, on beings suffering in this world; the embodiment of compassion, the greatest of the Bodhisattvas (*q.v.*).

Bliss body: See Sambhoga-kaya.

Bodhidharma: First patriarch of Ch'an (Zen) in China, who arrived there from India in the 6th century A.D.

Bodhisattva: A being of Enlightenment, whose nature it is to strive for the salvation of all sentient beings through wisdom and compassion.

Brahman: The supreme being of Hinduism, whose classical description is "*Neti, Neti*" ("not this, not that").

Caussade, J. P. de: 17th-century Jesuit authority on the spiritual life.

Cranmer, Thomas: A.D. 1489–1556, Archbishop of Canterbury.

Cyril of Alexandria: A.D. 376–444, Father of the Church who became Bishop of Alexandria and despite or perhaps because of his theological preoccupations, proved to be one of the less amiable Christian saints.

Dharma: A wide-ranging term impossible to pinpoint referring, according to its context, to universal truth, individual phenomena and, in particular, the Buddha's message.

Dharmakara: "Store of Dharma," Bodhisattva Dharmakara is said to have been the name of Amida prior to his attaining Buddhahood.

Dharma-kaya: Dharma body, the underlying principle of Mahayana Buddhism; the Buddha considered as the Absolute—from which emerge both the Sambhoga-kaya and the Nirmana-kaya (*qq.v.*).

Dogen: A.D. 1200–1253, one of the most famous Zen Masters. Leaving Japan, he spent five years in China. In later life, after his return, he founded Eihei-ji Temple, today the headquarters of the Soto school of Zen. He emphasized achieving Enlightenment by sitting meditation (Zazen).

Dogen Zenji: Formal title of Dogen.

Dokusan: A private meeting of an individual Zen meditant with his Roshi (teacher) during which the student conveys his understanding of his koan.

Eleusinian mysteries: Rites conducted at Eleusis, fourteen miles west of Athens, until the 4th century A.D. Some secret was allegedly disclosed to the initiates which was supposed to have had a comforting effect on "excited and believing minds."

Fudo-myo: "The Immobile One," the Bodhisattva who symbolizes the unvarying, unchanging. He is the embodiment of fearlessness and is characterized by detachment from passion and temptation. According to Japanese mythology, he was incarnated as a slave in order to serve all beings.

Gautama Buddha: See Sakyamuni.

Guru: Spiritual guide or preceptor.

Hakuin: The most outstanding Japanese Zen Master of the 18th century. He founded Ryutaku-ji, a monastery near Mishima City. One of his best-known aphorisms is: "This very place is the Lotus Land, this very body the Buddha."

Hannya-shin-gyo: Japanese abbreviation for the Prajna Paramita (transcendent wisdom) Hridaya Sutra. It is a primary source for understanding the background of Zen.

Heian-kyo: Kyoto. Founded in A.D. 794, it remained the capital of the Japanese empire for nearly eleven centuries.

Hinayana: Sanskrit for "the lesser vehicle" or "the lesser way," a term applied by the Mahayana (*q.v.*) school of Buddhism to those who hold the goal of Buddhism to be restricted to the Enlightenment of the individual.

Hoben: Japanese for the Sanskrit *Upaya,* whose meaning in context is "a temporary device for putting across a message."

Honen: Founder, in the 13th century, of the Jodo (Pure Land) sect of Japanese Buddhism.

Inka: Seal of approval, recognition by a Zen Master that a disciple has completed his training.

Ittoen: "The Garden of Light," one of the "new religions" founded in Japan by Nishida Tenko.

-ji: Japanese combining word meaning "monastery" or "temple."

Jodo: Pure Land.

Jodo-shin-shu: True Pure Land Sect; founded in Japan by Shinran (*q.v.*).

Joshu (Chinese: Chao-chu):   9th-century Chinese Ch'an (Zen) Master famous for his invention of the koan Mu (*q.v.*).

Kali: Hindu conception related to the god Shiva; a destructive, all-pervading time aspect known as the Power-of-Time.

Kamakura period: A.D. 1192–1333, a span of years during which Japan was largely governed by the Shogunate at Kamakura, a town near Tokyo.

Kami: Shinto term meaning "god spirit."

Karma: Action considered in relation to its inevitable consequences.

Karuna: Compassionate love.

Kegon sect: Sect of Japanese Buddhism founded by Genju-Daishi, a Chinese master (A.D. 643–712) and based on the Avatamsaka Sutra, of which the underlying theme is "One in all and all in one."

Keiken: The general experience of everyday life.

Kensho: Sudden Zen "Enlightenment" experience, or Satori, which need not necessarily be permanent.

Kitaro Nishida: Famous modern Japanese Buddhist philosopher (1870–1945), whose remains are venerated at Myoshin-ji, Kyoto. He is known for his philosophical theme of "Self-identity in Absolute contradictions."

Koan: An existential problem, often translated into a verbal puzzle, the solution of which is intended to lead the Zen disciple to Satori (Enlightenment). The Gen-jo koan arises from a living situation. Kosoku koan is one recorded in writing.

Kobo-Daishi: A.D. 774–835, founder in Japan of the Shingon-shu (*q.v.*) (True Word) sect of Esoteric, or Tantric, Buddhism.

Kodo Kyodan: "Filial Piety Church," a Japanese religious order, affiliated with the Tendai sect, founded by Shodo Okano.

Ku: Japanese for the Sanskrit *sunyata*, emptiness; a central Buddhist doctrine meaning that all phenomena are lacking in self-essence.

Madhyamika: The "middle way" between assertion and negation; a Buddhist dialectic associated with the philosopher Nagarjuna (*q.v.*).

Mahayana Buddhism: The Buddhism of "the greater vehicle" or "the greater way," a more highly elaborated and speculative form of Buddhism than the Hinayana (*q.v.*), which originated in India. Sometimes called the "Northern School of Buddhism," it took root notably in Tibet, China, Korea, and Japan.

Maitreya: The Buddha-yet-to-be, the personification of friendliness.

Mantra: A sacred sound usually verbalized, like the well-known Hindu mantra "Aum."

Meiji era: The period after 1868, when the government of Japan passed from the Shogunate to the Imperial Meiji household, which saw a whole series of reforms based on Western constitutional principles.

Metta: Friendliness or loving-kindness.

Mu: Japanese form of verbal negation. In the context of a koan (*q.v.*), however, it implies no absolute negative, but an invitation to the questioner to penetrate beyond appearances and the normal processes of rational thought to the underlying reality. Thus, the celebrated answer "*Mu*" to the question "Does a dog have the Buddha nature?" can only be understood when one has reached the heart of the Buddhist message.

Muso: Name by which the Zen Master Muso-Kokushi (1275–1351) is generally known.

Nagarjuna: Renowned Indian exponent of Buddhism in the 2nd century A.D. who was the founder of the Madhyamika school (*q.v.*).

Nara: Capital of Japan during the major part of the 8th century, when it was a chief center of Buddhism.

Nembutsu: See Pure Land.

Nichiren: 1222–1282, founder of the Japanese school of nationalistic Buddhism.

Nirmana-kaya: The "illusion" or "transformation body" of the Buddha; the appearance of the Dharma-kaya (*q.v.*) as a histori-

o

cal personage, *e.g.*, Sakyamuni, or as a manifestation of the Buddha.

Nirvana: The Buddhist meaning is defined in Webster's *New International Dictionary:* "The dying out in the heart of the threefold fire of *raga, dosa* and *moha*, or passion, hatred and delusion. This emancipation involves a beatific spiritual condition, and freedom from the necessity of future transmigration."

Obaku: A branch of the Zen school that combines the practice of chanting the Nembutsu with Zazen and koan training.

Pali texts: The oldest written Buddhist texts, codified by the Theravada (*q.v.*), or Southern, school. It is impossible to be even approximately certain about their dates, because the original documents, composed in India, have been lost there.

Paramitas: The way of practice of Buddhist virtues or perfections.

Prajna: The ultimate mind-heart wisdom practiced by those who are enlightened.

Puranas: Ancient Sanskrit writings of a legendary character embodying Hindu traditions.

Pure Land sect: The Jodo sect of Japanese Buddhism, founded by Honen in the 13th century. It was in part a reaction against the metaphysical and scholastic teaching that permeated contemporary Buddhism, and it focused attention on devotion to Amitabha (Amida) Buddha, as expressed in the Nembutsu (*Namu Amida Butsu*, Praise to Amida Buddha).

Rennyo: 15th-century exponent of Pure Land Buddhism.

Rinzai: In Chinese, Lin-chi, the founder of one of the two principle Zen schools, and the name of the school he founded, which was transmitted to Japan in 1191.

Rissho Kosei-Kai: "Society to Establish Righteousness and Foster Fellowship," a new Japanese religious movement of and for laymen, founded in 1938 in the Nichiren (*q.v.*) tradition and based on the Lotus Sutra.

Ruysbroeck, Jan Van: A.D. 1293–1381, Dutch mystic who taught the doctrine "The soul finds God in its own depths."

Sakyamuni: "Sage of the Sakya clan," Siddhartha Gautama, the historical Buddha, "the fully enlightened one," who lived in India possibly between 560 and 480 B.C.

Samadhi: Very deep meditative concentration resulting in a state of mental calm and absence of distractions.

Sambhoga-kaya: "Bliss body," one of the three aspects of the Buddha, the others being Dharma-kaya and Nirmana-kaya (*qq.v.*). Called also the "enjoyment body," it is a manifestation of the Dharma-kaya to the mind on its way to Enlightenment, bringing with it joy and a sense of exaltation.

Samsara: Process of birth and death; the round of existence where one phenomenon gives rise to another, like the successive waves of the sea.

Sanatana Dharma: "Eternal Religion," the Hindu belief that all the world religions, the several schools of Hinduism included, variously manifest one everlasting religion.

Sangha: Community of Buddhist initiates; also, one of the "three refuges," which are the Buddha, the Dharma, and the Sangha.

Sankara or **Sankaracarya:** One of the most celebrated Hindu theologians. He lived in India possibly in the 8th century A.D. and commented on the Upanishads (*q.v.*) and the Bhagavad-Gita, and greatly stressed the doctrine of Advaita (non-dualism).

Sensei: Teacher.

Sesshin: Searching the heart. Week-long periods of Zazen (*q.v.*), during which practitioners devote themselves to meditation and Dokusan (*q.v.*).

Shaktites: Devotees of the Hindu goddess Shakti, conceived as the embodiment of creative energy.

Shamanism: Form of priestly lore originating with the Ural-Altaic peoples and still a living force among some American Indians and in certain areas of Japan and Tibet.

Shingon-shu: Buddhist sect based principally on the teachings of the Mahavairocana Sutra, on the practice of mandala contemplation, and on the chanting of esoteric invocations. Shingon means mantra (*q.v.*).

Shinran: A.D. 1173–1262, the founder of the Jodo-shin sect.

Shinto: The ancient Japanese religion before the arrival of Buddhism. It means, literally, "the way of the gods," and its cult tends to identify the nation and its leaders with the divine order of things.

Shiva or **Siva:**   Hindu god representing the Divine Being in its negative aspect, often depicted as engaged in a dance of cosmic destruction.

Shobo Genzo: A work on Zen by Dogen (*q.v.*), the title of which may be translated "A Treasury of the Eye of the True Dharma."

Shogunate: Government under the direction of the highest-ranking military officer, the shogun, which functioned in Japan from 1192 to 1868.

Shukyo: Religion.

Skandhas: "Heaps" or "bundles." The five skandhas—the body, feelings, perceptions, impulses and emotions, and acts of consciousness—according to Buddhism go to make up the individual human being as viewed from the empirical level.

Soka Gakkai: "Value-creating Association," the best known of Japan's new religions.

Soto: One of the two principal schools of Japanese Zen—the other being Rinzai (*q.v.*)—founded by Dogen (*q.v.*), who emphasized Buddhist enlightenment in terms of sitting meditation (Zazen).

Sufi: Member of an Islamic religious order. The name derives from the white woolen robe worn by the initiated.

Sutra: Sanskrit for "thread," the name given to the Buddhist scriptures, the dialogues and sermons traditionally ascribed to Sakyamuni Buddha. The sutras, together with the vinaya (*q.v.*) and the abhidharma (*q.v.*), constitute the Tripitaka (three baskets), the recognized canon of Buddhist scriptures. Avatamsaka Sutra is one of the written sources for the Kegon (*q.v.*) sect.

Lotus Sutra, or Saddharma Pundarika Sutra, a Mahayana Buddhist text entitled "The Lotus of the Good Law," is one of the sources of inspiration for Soka Gakkai, as well as Tendai-shu and Nichiren-shu.

Nirvana Sutra is one of the written sources for Pure Land Buddhism.

Prajna Paramita Sutra is the Transcendental Wisdom Sutra, uniquely important as one of the sources of Zen.

Sukhavati Vyuha Sutra, the Array of the Blissful Land Sutra, is one of the texts to which the Pure Land sect appeals.

Yogacara Sutra is probably a reference to the Lankavatara Sutra, which expounds the "mind only" doctrine characteristic of the Yogacara (*q.v.*) school.

Taiken: An individual's personal experience.

Tantrism: A form of esoteric Buddhism involving the use of highly complex, though potentially illuminating, symbolism. Tantra means thread, loom, or warp, and so implies, in practice, "obtaining the inner essence."

Tendai-shu: School of Japanese Buddhism founded in the 9th century by Dengyo-Daishi (767–822).

Theravada: "The Way of the Elders," the southern Buddhist school prevailing chiefly in Ceylon, Burma, and Southeast Asia.

Tri-kaya: The "three bodies" of the Buddha: Dharma-kaya, Sambhoga-kaya, and Nirmana-kaya (*qq.v.*).

Upanishads: Inspired writings, originally in Sanskrit, which with the Vedas and the Bhagavad-Gita are the recognized sources of Hinduism.

Upaya: "Skill in Means," the employment, motivated by compassion, of some expository device adapted to the receptive capacity of the learner.

Vajrayana: "The Diamond Way," a concept deriving from Tantrism (*q.v.*) that connotes the adamantine quality of a thunderbolt. Expressed in myth and ritual, the path to Enlightenment opens before the devotee.

Vasubandhu: 5th-century-A.D. exponent of Buddhism and cofounder, with his brother Asanga, of the Yogacara (*q.v.*) school.

Vinaya: The rules for Buddhist monastic discipline, which number, according to different schools, 250 or 348.

Vishnu: Hindu god manifesting the Divine under the aspect of pervader, sustainer, or preserver of the cosmos.

Yang-Yin: The positive-negative polarization under which Chinese philosophers have viewed the cosmos; *e.g.*, male-female, light-darkness, fire-water.

Yogacara: Highly intellectual school of Buddhism known as the "mind only" school, roughly equivalent to subjective idealism. It was founded at the beginning of the 5th century A.D. by Asanga and Vasubandhu, natives of northwest India.

Zazen: Sitting meditation.

Zendo: Zen meditation hall.

Index

(An asterisk indicates that the entry is to be found in the glossary of "Some Terms and Names That May Call for Explanation," pp. 189–98.)